END GAME
BURMA

END GAME BURMA

Slim's master stroke, Meiktila 1945

MICHAEL PEARSON

Pen & Sword
MILITARY

First published in Great Britain in 2010 by
PEN & SWORD MILITARY
An imprint of
Pen & Sword Books Ltd
47 Church Street
Barnsley
South Yorkshire
S70 2AS

Copyright © Michael Pearson, 2010

ISBN 978-1-84884-114-7

A CIP catalogue record for this book is
available from the British Library

Typeset by Concept, Huddersfield, West Yorkshire
Printed and bound in England by the MPG Books Group.

Pen & Sword Books Ltd incorporates the Imprints of Pen & Sword Aviation,
Pen & Sword Maritime, Pen & Sword Military, Wharncliffe Local History,
Pen & Sword Select, Pen & Sword Military Classics, Leo Cooper,
Remember When, Seaforth Publishing and Frontline Publishing

For a complete list of Pen & Sword titles please contact
PEN & SWORD BOOKS LIMITED
47 Church Street, Barnsley, South Yorkshire, S70 2AS, England
E-mail: enquiries@pen-and-sword.co.uk
Website: www.pen-and-sword.co.uk

Those struggling along the road were almost all in their twenties, yet they stooped like old men ... Nobody could have believed that these men had once possessed the strength to survive a series of intense battles ...

When confronted by the actual scenes I was not moved to tears, perhaps owing to my youth or the fact that I had an unsentimental view of the war in those days. But I do not have the same unsentimental view now, nor am I young any longer. Now I can freely cry over my friends who died.

Former Staff Sergeant Yasumasa Nishiji,
20th Independent Engineering Regiment

Contents

Note: For ease of identification Japanese units and those of their allies are given in *italics*.

List of Plates

Lieutenant General Masaki Honda, Commander 33rd Army (right), with Lieutenant General Hayashi (left) and Major General Koba.

Field Marshal Count Juichi Terauchi, Japanese Supreme Commander South East Asia and Admiral Mountbatten's opposite number.

3-inch mortars in action amid the pagodas of Meiktila.

Japanese attack on the cantonment area of Meiktila. Some of the 281 bodies counted the morning after the attack.

The wreckage of Meiktila railway station, focus for a number of hard fought actions.

A British infantryman cautiously approaches a Japanese foxhole on the outskirts of Meiktila.

Some of the few Allied landing craft left in theatre land XV Corps troops and equipment during the vital capture of Ramree Island.

Assault landing craft of the Indian Navy beaching in a narrow chaung in the Ru-Ywa area of the Arakan.

Battle scarred street in the Fort Dufferin area of Mandalay.

The road from Mandalay. Ground crew 152 Squadron, RAF, leave Mandalay for Meiktila and Rangoon.

Yewe Village near Yindan, 12 miles S.E. of Meiktila. Troops move cautiously forward, tree to tree over bullet-swept ground, as a tank blasts a Japanese foxhole at point-blank range.

Monsoon. Digging drainage ditches in an attempt to keep torrential downpours from flooding the campsite.

Native style 'basha' hut adopted by Allied servicemen in Burma.

Transshipment of ammunition, Dakota transport to truck at a forward airstrip.

Reconnaissance photograph of Meiktila taken 30 January 1945.

Acknowledgements

The Imperial War Museum Photographic Archive, London.

The Library of Congress, Washington DC.

The National Archive, Kew.

The National Archives and Records Administration, Modern Military Branch, Maryland, USA.

Mrs Carol Toone-Hollis (nee White) for her kind permission to use photographs and anecdotes from her father's records.

List of Abbreviations

ABDACOM	American, British, Dutch and Australian Command
AHQ	Air Headquarters
ALFSEA	Allied Land Forces South East Asia
CCTF	Combat Cargo Task Force
EAC	Eastern Air Command
GOC	General Officer Commanding
HQ	Headquarters
INA	Indian National Army
JAAF	Japanese Army Air Force
NCAC	Northern Combat Area Command
PBF	Patriotic Burmese Forces
RAF	Royal Air Force
RN	Royal Navy
SACSEA	Supreme Allied Command South East Asia
SEAC	South East Asia Command
USAAF	United States Army Air Force

Maps

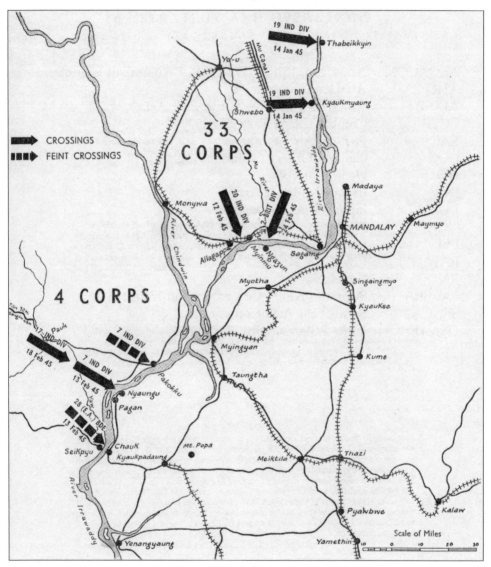

Map 1. XXXIII Corps and IV Corps, the Irrawaddy crossings.

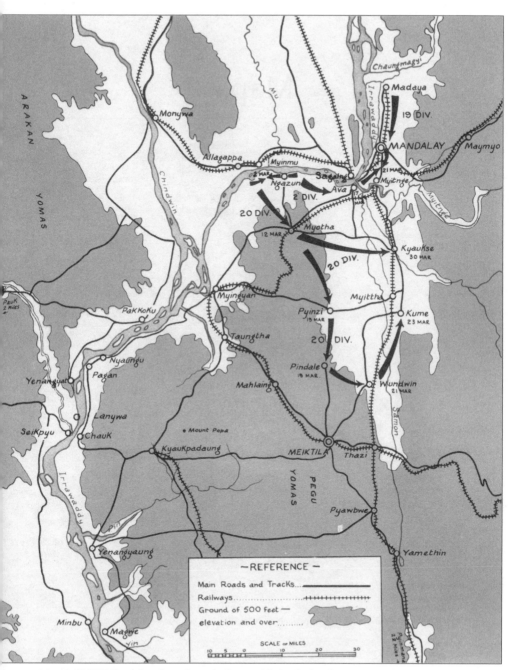

Map 2. XXXIII Corps breakout from the Irrawaddy bridgeheads.

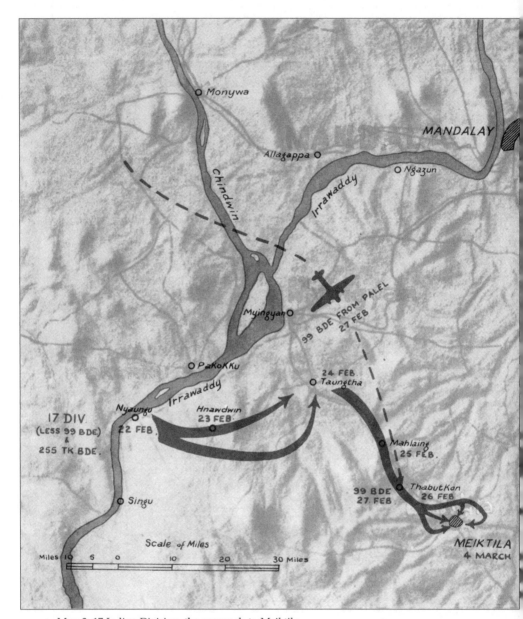

Map 3. 17 Indian Division, the approach to Meiktila.

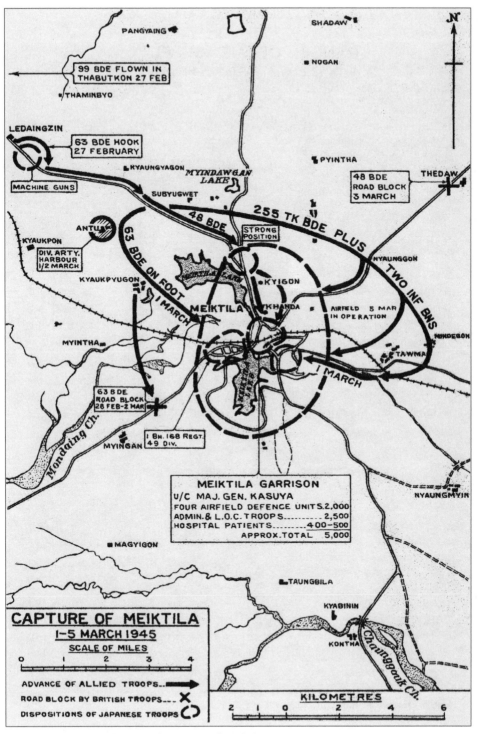

Map 4. 17 Indian Division, the capture of Meiktila.

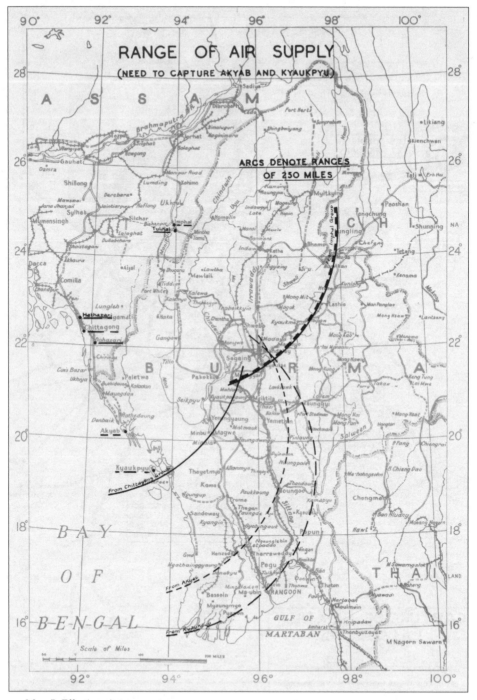

Map 5. Effective air transport range.

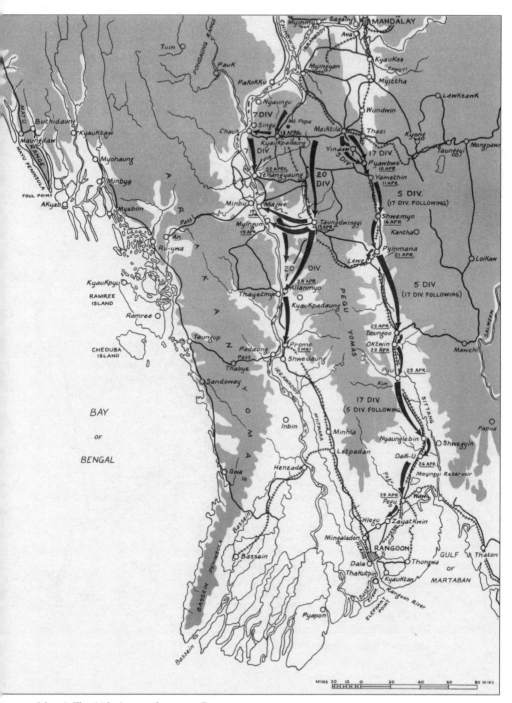

Map 6. The 14th Army advance to Rangoon.

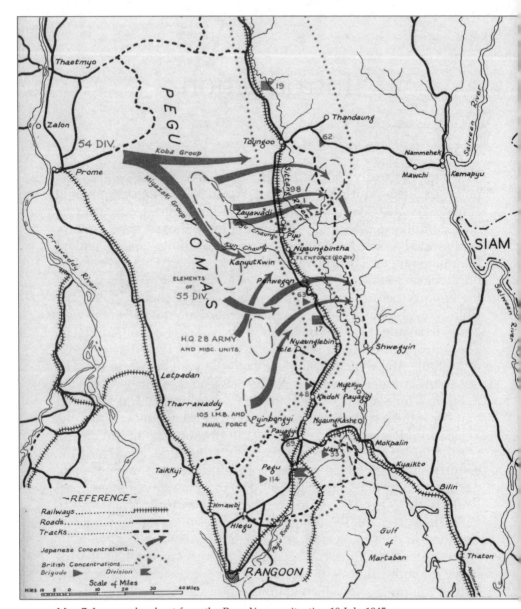

Map 7. Japanese breakout from the Pegu Yomas, situation 19 July 1945.

Introduction

Two factors greatly influenced the distinctive nature of the campaign in Burma during the Second World War – topography and climate. At 240,000 square miles (386,241 km^2) Burma covers a vast area comprised principally of mountainous jungle. The country is dissected north to south by four major rivers and attendant mountain ranges. The Irrawaddy River rises in the Himalayas to the north, close to Fort Hertz, and runs southward down the spine of the country across a dry central plain to the Rangoon delta. The Chindwin also has its source in the northern mountains, to the west of the Irrawaddy, joining the latter at Pakkoku, south of Mandalay. The source of the Sittang lies to the east of the Irrawaddy, just south of Meiktila, the river running south to the Gulf of Martaban. The last of the country's great rivers, the Salween, lies further east still, rising in China and dissecting the 3,000 feet high (914m) tableland that constitutes eastern Burma, the river subsequently crossing the Tenasserim Peninsula to reach the Gulf of Martaban at Moulmein.

All four rivers have numerous tributaries that criss-cross the country, most of which formed a serious obstacle to movement during the Burma Campaign, as did the mountain ranges, particularly the Naga Hills along the border with India which rise to 12,000 feet (3,657m). To add to the difficulties these ranges would be sheathed in dense jungle up to a height of 6,000 feet (1,828m).

The climate in Burma is generally more equable than that of India, the more mountainous country not being subject to the long, hot, dry summers to which southern India in particular is prone. However, Burma does have a monsoon season starting in April, continuing through to mid September and affecting the entire country with the exception of the previously mentioned central plain around Mandalay and Meiktila. During the monsoon, rivers, valleys and flat areas flood and keeping anything dry, such as clothes, bedding and equipment, is virtually impossible and health suffers as a result. In the 1940s disease associated with unclean water was rampant, British and Allied forces reporting 250,000 cases of malaria and dysentery in the year 1943/44 alone.

A further hindrance to effective campaigning was the road system, primitive in the extreme, and comprising for the most part little more than dirt tracks. The main all weather roads ran from Rangoon to Mandalay, from Meiktila through the Shan State, and from Toungoo through the Karen Hills to Loilem.

The relentless march of technology inevitably transforms the demands and requirements placed upon generals in command of large forces, and while arguably offering more options to those lucky enough to be able to reap its benefits, alters both the strategy and tactics that they employ. However, for the campaign to capture Meiktila, Lieutenant General Slim (later Field Marshal Viscount) combined superb use of the cutting-edge technology of the time, notably air power and armour, with a consummate tactical virtuosity that would have been recognisable to both Napoleon Bonaparte and Julius Caesar.

14 December 1941 saw the opening of the Japanese campaign to capture Burma and a mere six months later that campaign was complete, what remained of the defenders being bundled uncer-emoniously across the north-western border into India, an invidious end to the longest retreat in British military history. It is true that the defenders were outnumbered and poorly equipped, however it is also true to say that they were disastrously unprepared, outfought, and out-generalled; their basic strategy of tying themselves to motorised columns being completely unsuited to a vast country that comprised virtually all mountainous jungle with few metalled roads and little relatively flat terrain on which those motorised columns might be successfully deployed. Placed in command of Burcorps (as the defence force came to be named) in March 1942, Slim led his battered command out of Burma into India, learned the lessons well and, with others, began a quest to develop a viable plan to re-take the country.

Chapter 1

Learning the Lessons

I

William Joseph Slim was a rarity in the British Army of the early 20th century, a man born of relatively humble beginnings who rose to the very top of his chosen profession. The reason for a preponderance of well-to-do senior ranks is not difficult to discern as the Army at that time did not financially support officers in training. Nevertheless, born October 1891, the son of an iron merchant in Bristol, Slim set his heart on a military career despite the fact that he simply did not have the necessary financial backing to pursue his ambition to become an officer. With his path to career advancement a potentially rocky one, he went as far as he could and became a member of the University Officer Training Corps, an organisation offering training in leadership and basic military skills to those students who might seek a commission in the Territorial Army (somewhat unflatteringly, and unfairly, termed 'weekend soldiers' by the Regular Army).

Unable to progress further, on leaving school Slim worked variously as a clerk, teacher, and foreman at an engineering firm; however his potentially stillborn future in the military was rescued by the outbreak of the First World War when he (together with another future British General of the Second World War, Bernard Law Montgomery) was commissioned into the Royal Warwickshire (Territorial) Regiment.

Slim was wounded at both Gallipoli and Mesopotamia (where he was awarded the Military Cross), and on the cessation of hostilities transferred to the Indian Army where he gained a permanent commission. By 1940, and with the rank of Brigadier, Slim commanded 10 Indian Infantry Brigade in Abyssinia, a campaign that did not go particularly well for him, not least because he was once again wounded.

1

In June 1941, as Chief of Staff, Slim accompanied the Expeditionary Force to Syria. Within days of the opening of the campaign the Officer Commanding 10 Indian Division fell ill and Slim replaced him, proving successful at that level of command. Promoted Lieutenant General in March 1942, he was sent to Burma to command Burcorps, then in the process of being badly mauled by the Japanese. Without the men or resources to turn the tide, Slim prevented what was in danger of degenerating into a disorderly panic and conducted an ordered withdrawal of some 900 miles (1,448km) into India.

Not being a showman like Montgomery, Slim was nevertheless mentally strong, of equable temperament, and possessed of an imposing physical presence that inspired confidence. He also, perhaps as a result of his own modest upbringing, possessed a 'common touch' that enabled him to communicate with the men under his command in a manner that they understood, and in the multi-national 14th Army in Burma often in their own language be it English, Gurkhali, or Urdu. In 1948 Slim was promoted Field Marshal and became Chief of the Imperial General Staff.

On the Japanese side of the hill, following the disastrous defeat at Slim's hands at Imphal and Kohima Burma Area Army Commander Masakazu Kawabe was replaced by Heitaro Kimura, and as the critical battle for Meiktila developed Kimura gave Masaki Honda battlefield command in an attempt to turn back 14th Army's offensive. Kimura was born in September 1888 and attended military school from an early age, graduating from the Imperial Japanese Army Academy in 1908 and the Army War College in 1916, being commissioned into the artillery.

Kimura saw active service during the Japanese intervention in Russia 1918–1919, from the late 1920s was attached to the Inspectorate of Artillery and was an instructor at the Field Artillery School. An appointment to the Japanese delegation to the London Disarmament Conference of 1929–1931 was followed by promotion to lieutenant colonel and further artillery postings.

Kimura's stature and influence grew and promotions followed – major general in 1936, lieutenant general in 1939 and combat command of the *32nd Division* in China 1939–1940. From 1940 to 1941 Kimura served as Chief of Staff to the powerful and influential Kwangtung Army in Manchukuo.

On his return to Japan in 1941 Kimura served as Vice Minister of War, assisting War Minister Hideki Tojo develop plans for the continuation of the Sino-Japanese War and prosecution of the impending Pacific War. From 1943 to 1944 Kimura was a member of the Supreme War Council, but as the war in Burma began to go against Japan, found himself despatched to field command there in an attempt to redress the situation. Captured by Allied forces at the end of the war, Kimura was accused of failing to prevent atrocities against prisoners of war and with complicity in the abuse and deaths of civilian and military prisoners on the Burma Railway. Found guilty by the International Military Tribunal for the Far East he was hanged in 1948 as a war criminal.

Masaki Honda was born in 1889, the son of a former retainer to the powerful Iida clan now working as a minor civil servant. Honda entered the local school at Nagano, but his father seems to have had military ambitions for the boy and quickly transferred him to the Military Academy where he passed out in 1910 and was gazetted sub-lieutenant in the 4th Regiment of the Imperial Guards Division.

Honda became something of an academic in the Imperial Japanese Army, a fact that was recognised by his appointment in 1930 as senior lecturer at the Infantry School and his appointment in 1932 to the Military Education Branch. Promoted major-general, in 1938 he became second in command at the Infantry School, a highly significant posting with war in the air and tactics for the Imperial Japanese Army being thrashed out in preparation for the conflict that would inevitably come.

In December 1939 Honda obtained the rank of lieutenant general and a posting to the Chinese Expeditionary Army as Chief of Staff. Field commands followed as GOC *8th Division* in 1940, and *20th Army* in Manchukuo in 1943, before taking up his final military appointment as commander of *33rd Army* in Burma.

Honda was not an extrovertly dashing character and was generally respected and liked by the men under his command without being unduly popular. Apart from military matters he loved fishing, drinking *sake*, and telling jokes which, although apparently very amusing, tended to become more and more obscene the more the situation on the battlefield degenerated. Masaki Honda survived the war and died in 1964.

3

II

In their campaign to capture Burma the Japanese used the jungle to their advantage, utilising a wide flanking or 'hook' tactic that they were to employ with great effect in all their campaigns across the Far East. The largely British-led Indian Army formed the backbone of the Allied forces in Burma in 1941 and would to continue to do so until the country's final recapture from Japan in 1945. The Indian Army was trained, as was the British Army and all the armies of the western industrialised nations, to use armoured units to smash through enemy defences, closely followed by infantry support. Motorised columns were used extensively to transport food, ammunition, and other essentials rapidly to the front in order to exploit any opening in the enemy defences with the minimum of delay, the lesson of the First World War in Europe being that any breakthrough soon withered and died without rapid replenishment and reinforcement. The German 'blitzkrieg' was the ultimate refinement of this method, however it was a method that required metalled roads and relatively open country, and was therefore totally unsuited to the topography of Burma.

Finding themselves anchored to their transport columns in a vast mountainous country of few suitable roads, the defence forces in Burma in 1941/42 were easy prey to attack from the highly effective Japanese Army Air Force, while Japanese infantry quickly adapted to jungle warfare, travelled light, and were not hampered by reliance on motorised transport, using bicycles where necessary and living by turns off captured enemy rations or the jungle itself.

Thus unhindered, the Japanese were able to infiltrate jungle terrain that to their opponents seemed impenetrable, emerging without warning, setting up roadblocks and cutting their enemy off from supplies and reinforcement. Being surrounded in such an inhospitable environment was not a pleasant experience, and in those early battles the invariable response of the defence was a hurried retreat to remove the roadblocks in their rear, at which point the Japanese would initiate a further 'hook' and another Allied retreat would be the inevitable result.

Being the consummate professional that he was, the then Lieutenant General William Slim realized the need to accumulate as much information as possible on the Japanese military and its methods, and that entailed meeting primarily with the Chinese, who had been at war with Japan since 1931 in disputed Manchuria, and in China itself since 1937.

Appreciating the need to keep the vitally important Burma supply road open, in December 1941 Generalissimo Chiang Kai-shek offered the Chinese 5th and 6th armies[1] for the defence of Burma. Such reinforcement was very welcome, but all too soon they were pushed back, in their case north-eastwards into China, while the Anglo-Indian defenders were sent packing north-westwards into India. However, one vitally important outcome of the Chinese involvement was that Slim did get the chance to attend a number of conferences at which he was able to meet Chinese officers, one of whom, it transpired, had played a leading part in China's victory over the Japanese at Changsha. Drawing the general aside, Slim, via an interpreter, questioned him closely. In this officer's experience so confident of victory were the Japanese that they operated to very tight logistical limits, usually carrying into an attack supplies sufficient for nine days only. This applied not only to food but also to ammunition and equipment, the Japanese relying on being able to obtain replenishment from captured enemy stores as they advanced. If, the Chinese general believed, the Japanese could be denied this captured replenishment for longer than nine days, and then subjected to determined counter-attack, it could well be possible to defeat them. This was exactly the sort of background information that Slim sought and he took note of it for future reference, but remained profoundly aware that it offered no panacea, not least since the Chinese themselves had found it impossible to repeat their Changsha success elsewhere.

With Burma lost, British commanders faced the problem not only of how to regain the offensive, but how to prevent the Japanese from pushing further into India, for in 1942 Mahatma Gandhi (although not interested in replacing British occupation with Japanese) actively agitated for independence from Britain, and the vast Indian sub-continent must have appeared to the Japanese High Command like fruit ripe and ready for the picking.

Reflecting on the campaign just past, Slim had been impressed by the aggressive singleness of purpose of the Japanese commanders, their sole aim the rapid destruction of all enemy formations opposing them. By contrast the British command, evidently bemused from the outset by the speed with which events overtook them, clung to a vague notion to hold on to territory, which, Slim later wrote, 'led to the initial dispersion of our forces over wide areas, an error which we continued to commit, and worse still it led to a defensive attitude of mind'.[2]

At a conference in Washington in December 1941, shortly after the commencement of hostilities by Japan, the principal Far Eastern Allies, America, Britain, the Netherlands, and Australia, met to agree a mutually supportive plan of action. The result was the formation of a new joint command structure, designated ABDACOM, which would have principal responsibility for all areas of the Far East, with the notable exception of the Pacific which then, as later in the war, proved to be a delicate subject with some elements in the US command. However, in these early days the arrangement also made sound military sense as campaigning in the Pacific would by definition be a largely naval affair, and the Allies only other major naval power, Britain, had its hands full in the Atlantic and the Mediterranean.

Under the auspices of ABDACOM General Sir Archibald Wavell became C-in-C Far East, while Air Marshal Sir Richard Peirse took command of all Allied air forces, and by mid 1942, General Wavell, now C-in-C India, had initiated discussions on prospects for the re-conquest of Burma. As he and his colleagues (including Lieutenant General Slim) saw it, there were two possibilities for a full blown invasion: (1) from the sea in the Rangoon area; and (2) land based, from India, across the mountains to the north and down the Irrawaddy valley to Rangoon. Over time, various plans for a sea borne invasion were drawn up, only to be subsequently discarded due to a chronic lack of landing craft. As the war progressed this shortage became ever more acute as landing craft of all types and sizes were returned to Britain to take part in the Normandy landings. In fact, for more or less the entire duration of the war Burma languished at the bottom of the priority list for reinforcements, arms, equipment, and supplies of all types. The problem was not just a shortage of men and equipment, but a worldwide shortage of ships in which to carry them. Europe, North Africa, and later the campaign in Italy, inevitably took precedence.

Without landing craft, an invasion overland from the north was the only viable alternative, the glaring problem being the long supply line stretching across India into Burma that would be required to keep an army on the move. Allied troops in Assam, along the border with Burma, could only be reached, circuitously, by rail or river – no roads worthy of the name existed.

From the main port at Calcutta a broad gauge railway, approximately half of which was single track only, ran for 235 miles (378km) to Parbatipur. Here gangs of coolies manually transferred freight to a train on the decrepit metre-gauge line that would (hopefully) be waiting to take the goods on a further rambling 200-plus mile ride to the ferry at Pandu where railway wagons and coaches were uncoupled and manually pushed onto barges for a laborious river crossing. On the far side the train would be reassembled and proceed for a further 200-plus serpentine miles to the terminus for the Central Front at Dimapur, over 600 miles (966km) from Calcutta. For the Northern Front, freight had an additional 200 clanking, groaning rail miles to travel to Ledo.

Built to transport tea from the plantations in Assam, peacetime capacity for the railway was 600 tons per day. With the formation of 14th Army this rose to 2,800 tons, a still perfectly inadequate amount to supply both British and Commonwealth forces at Imphal and the Chinese at Ledo. With no additional experienced personnel available from either India or Britain, the US Army stepped into the breach with six battalions of Railway Troops – 4,700 fully trained railwaymen. By October 1944 daily capacity had risen to 4,400 tons.

The problems did not end in Assam for to cross the trackless Naga Hills into Burma any invading force would be required to build a supply road as it advanced, with all the drain on manpower and resources that implies. There did, however, exist an alternative (at that time admittedly radical in the extreme) to the problematical construction of a supply road but in mid 1942 none of the senior commanders seem to have seriously considered it. None, that is, with the exception of Air Vice Marshal A.C. Collier, Air Officer Administration, AHQ India, who, commenting on an Air Staff planning paper, on 14 July 1942 wrote:

It is surprising to see no mention of transport aircraft for the solution of supply problems during the initial stage of an advance into Burma. In my opinion, the success or failure of

7

operations ... in this communicationless area would depend very largely on the intelligent use of transport aircraft.[3]

To put these comments into perspective it should be remembered that in 1942 the use of air power was still very much in its infancy, and the large scale air supply of army-sized formations so far off the radar that the RAF did not feel the need to build its own transport aircraft, opting instead to purchase what it needed from the United States. On the outbreak of hostilities with Japan, six months prior to Air Vice Marshal Collier putting pen to paper, the entire RAF transport strength in the whole of India/Burma amounted to two – aircraft, that is, not squadrons. These were two Douglas DC2s belonging to 31 Squadron, probably the most experienced transport squadron in the RAF, and at that time split between duties in the Middle East and the two aircraft in India. However even this tiny establishment was soon reduced to one, the second aircraft being destroyed in January 1942 during a Japanese air raid on Mingaladon, one of the Rangoon airfields.

It would take time, but from Air Vice Marshal Collier's insightful comments would develop one of the most innovative campaigns in military history, with the desperate battles for Meiktila its finale.

III

Although for the most part close allies during the Second World War and since the strategic objectives of Britain and the United States have often differed substantially, and this was certainly the case with Burma. Initially, American interest centred on keeping the Burma Road, which wound its toruous way northwards from Rangoon into China, open to supply Chinese armies, for the very good reason that if China were to be defeated substantial numbers of combat hardened Japanese troops would be released for service in the Pacific. With Burma lost, the United States shifted emphasis to bringing supplies by road across India from Calcutta and Karachi to air bases in north eastern India, then flying them across the Himalayas into China – 'flying The Hump' the aircrew called it – and an exceptionally hazardous undertaking it proved to be.

Keeping China in the war was essential to both Britain and the United States, and as a consequence Generalissimo Chiang Kai-shek was appointed Supreme Allied Commander in the China Theatre (a largely cosmetic device since he commanded in China with or without the grandiose title). The US Army's Lieutenant General Joseph Stilwell became both deputy commander in China under Chiang, and Allied Chief of Staff. It is fair to say that the Chinese soldiery was not highly regarded in most military circles. Nevertheless, Stillwell became an impassioned supporter and believed that, properly trained and equipped, they could be a decisive weapon. He also championed an alternative to 'The Hump' in the form of a road to be built from Assam in north eastern India, via Ledo in northern Burma, to Kunming in China.

Both the airlift from India and construction of the Ledo Road required agreement with Great Britain, the colonial power, but the United States had no interest in the reconquest of Burma itself.

The British position was almost exactly the opposite – Churchill dissenting, preferring a 'third way', an attack on the island of Sumatra upon which air bases could be established. Agreeing that the Chinese should be kept supplied to keep them in the war, but with little faith in the ability of Chiang Kai-shek or his forces to mount a sustained and effective attack, the British favoured defeating the Japanese in Burma and reopening the Burma Road from Rangoon. They of course also intended returning Burma and Malaya to the British Empire, which was precisely what the United States most strongly objected to.

One thing that Britain and the United States did agree on was that the command structure in India/Burma needed a drastic overhaul. At the time of the Japanese invasion of Malaya/Burma overall command of the defence rested with Britain's C-in-C India, however Prime Minister Churchill proposed a split, with C-in-C India left to oversee the governance of that vast country, while military operations against the Japanese became the responsibility of an entirely new formation.

In August 1943 Prime Minister Churchill, together with his Chiefs of Staff, sailed aboard the *Queen Mary* to Halifax, Nova Scotia, to meet with US President Roosevelt. The principal reason for the conference was to discuss Operation Overlord, the impending Allied invasion of Europe but also high on the list was India/Burma, and in this respect agreement was reached concerning the formation of South East Asia Command (SEAC) with Admiral Lord Louis Mountbatten as Supreme Allied Commander in that theatre.

Mountbatten had seen military service with the Royal Navy in the First World War, and in 1939 became became Captain (D) of the 5th Destroyer Flotilla, with HMS *Kelly* as his flagship. Mountbatten's career aboard *Kelly* was certainly spectacular, and brought him to the attention of Churchill, whose liking for 'men of action' was well known. At the time of his elevation to Supreme Commander SEAC Mountbatten had received brevet promotions to Admiral but, surprisingly, the fact remains that he was still only 43 years of age and held the substantive rank of Captain, RN.

Crucially, Mountbatten was well liked by the US Administration, an important factor since he would have US formations, principally USAAF, under command. Despite many difficulties he proved to be an excellent choice, not least as a result of his ability to get a disparate and prickly collection of subordinates to work successfully together.

Another of Churchill's 'men of action', Brigadier Orde Wingate, commander of the 'Chindit' guerrilla formations, also accompanied Churchill to Canada aboard *Queen Mary*, and greatly impressed the Prime Minister, to the extent that Churchill wanted him for command of land forces in India/Burma. Wingate had undoubted military qualities, but whether he had the experience and, perhaps more importantly, the temperament for such an important post must remain an open question. Ultimately, in October 1943, command of the newly formed 14th Army, comprising at that time the Indian IV and XV Corps, went to William Slim, who was to become one of the most successful Allied generals of the war. The 14th Army was itself part of 11th Army Group under the command of General Sir George Giffard.

Slim's problems on taking command were daunting, notably in the area of supply. The main depot for the central front in Dimapur, Assam, should have held 65,000 tons but in fact contained 47,000 tons, and that critically deficient in fresh meat and vegetables. To make matters worse his British and Indian soldiery required entirely different rations – the 14th Army had thirty different ration requirements, based largely on religion or district of origin. In a country almost totally devoid of either cold storage facilities or refrigerator trucks and railway wagons, the result was a diet of 'bully' (canned salted beef) and little else, with an impact on the health of the men that served to exacerbate the detrimental effects of climate, insects, and unclean water. In 1943, for every man evacuated as a battle casualty, 120 were evacuated sick.

Slim set to with a will and began the task of bringing some improvement to the situation, but what he needed was time. However, although not as yet aware of it, time was another precious commodity that he was very short of.

IV

Despite initial heady success, as the year 1943 moved toward its conclusion, the Japanese High Command began to appreciate that as things stood they were not about to achieve the quick victory over the Western Allies that they desperately needed in order to continue full-blown prosecution of their invasion of China; a colonial war essential to their expansionist aims as that vast country contained much of the raw material that Japan itself lacked but critically required in order to feed its industrialised war economy.

To complicate matters, Japanese merchant shipping losses in the Pacific mounted alarmingly, raising the prospect that the armies maintaining Japan's now far-flung empire might shortly face slow strangulation for want of supply and reinforcement. What was needed, the High Command reasoned, was a decisive victory that would irrevocably alter the course of the war in their favour, and their gaze settled upon Assam in north-eastern India. Having already beaten the British/Indian army in Burma with some ease, an invasion from that country into Assam held promise of stunning results – the 'Hump' supply route would be cut and, they reasoned, China would not long survive without American aid. Additionally, and although it was not a prime objective, there was always the possibility that, given the right circumstances, India itself might fall into their grasp.

The plan finally agreed upon was presented to (and according to some accounts originally conceived by) Lieutenant General Renya Mutaguchi for implementation. Under the plan, Mutaguchi took command of the *15th Army*, facing IV Corps on the Imphal Plain in Assam, while two new Japanese Armies were formed, the *28th Army* under Lieutenant General Shozo Sakurai, to open an offensive against XV Corps in the Arakan specifically to draw reinforcements away from Assam, and the *33rd Army*, under the command of Lieutenant General Masaki Honda, to halt the progress of General

11

Stillwell's Chinese divisions advancing from the north. These three armies together formed the Burma Area Army of Lieutenant General Kawabe. Lieutenant General Shozo was to open the campaign with his offensive in the Arakan, scheduled for the first week in February 1944.

On the Allied side, much had changed since the disasters of 1942. Training and equipment were much improved, both a boost for the all-important morale of the men, which was given an additional fillip by the apparent success of Wingate's first Chindit operation. In strict military terms this had not been the success hoped for, however the attendant, and positive, press coverage helped begin to dispel a growing impression that, in jungle warfare, the Japanese were superhuman 'bogeymen'.

There was one other pivotal development for the Allies, the growth of their air forces. Fighters, bombers, and the all-important transport aircraft were now much more in evidence. There were not nearly enough – there never would be – but there were enough for General Slim to issue an edict to his command to the effect that if, in future campaigns, the Japanese used their familiar 'hook' tactic, Allied troops were not to retreat as previously, but were to dig in, deny their supplies and equipment to the enemy, and themselves be supplied from the air until they could be reinforced or fight their way out. It was an instruction that would soon be put to the test.

Slim's strategy was originally, and characteristically, offensive in nature and as a result Lieutenant General Christison's XV Corps, comprising 5 and 7 Indian Divisions, began an advance in the Arakan commencing 30 November 1943. Initially the advance went slowly as the Corps fought its way down the Mayu Peninsula, which stretches southward for some 90 miles from Cox's Bazaar before tapering to a point suggesting an exclamation mark, with Akyab Island as the full stop. Along the spine the jungle covered ridge that comprises the Mayu Range juts upward to a height of 1,000–2,000 feet (304–609m), while narrow, low lying coastal strips border the Bay of Bengal on the western side of the peninsula, and the Mayu River to the east.

Only one road crossed the Mayu Peninsula, that from the small port of Maungdaw on the western coast, across to Buthidaung in the valley of the Kalapanzin River. Some 5 miles to the north, however, a narrow footpath crossed through the Ngakyedauk Pass.

Christison had his Corps disposed with 7 Division to the east of the Mayu Range, and 5 Division along the crest and on the western side. In January 1944 Maungdaw was captured and put in shape to receive supplies, but with the daunting Razabil fortress and Buthidaung both still in Japanese hands, it was still not possible to use the road across the Mayu. To counter the effects of this to some extent 7 Division engineers constructed an unmetalled road of their own across the Ngakyedauk Pass, and a maintenance area comprising supply depots, ammunition dumps, vehicle parks and dressing stations, was established on the eastern side at Sinzeweya. A decision was duly taken to bypass Razabil in the west and attack Buthidaung from the eastern side of the peninsula, and reinforcements duly tramped across Ngakyedauk and marched away south for the purpose. It was at this point, the morning of 4 February, that Lieutenant General Shozo launched his attack.

Slim was expecting such an attack, and planned for it, but admits that the timing took him completely by surprise. Shozo concealed the movement of his divisions with great skill and when they debouched from the jungle 5–6 miles in rear of 7 Division and only 2–3 miles from Ngakyedauk, Christison faced the disastrous possibility that if Japanese forces took the Pass his Corps might be defeated in detail, its two divisions unable to support each other, separated as they were by the impassable Mayu Range. At the time that Shozo attacked nothing lay between him and a truly stunning victory save the maintenance and administration area at Sinzeweya, the 'Admin Box'.

Lieutenant General Messervy, GOC 7 Division, had established his headquarters some 3 miles to the north-east of the administration area, and directly in the path of the oncoming Japanese. Having sent all available troops forward for the attack on Buthidaung, he and his HQ staff were obliged to conduct a fighting retreat to Sinzeweya, where they found that, as Slim had instructed, the largely admin staff, medics, and mechanics based there had not retreated but were dug in awaiting the oncoming attack.

The battle of the 'Admin Box' continued for seventeen days, the surrounded defenders being supplied and reinforced by air. The critical period was 7–20 February during which RAF and USAAF transport aircraft flew 639 sorties, and their fighter escorts flew 342. A feature of the supply operation was the dropping, in addition to

13

military supplies, of cigarettes and the new SEAC newspaper, with the express purpose of fostering in the men on the ground a belief that, while their situation might be serious, it was temporary and not in the least hopeless.

The 'Admin Box' not only held, but, combined with reinforcements from the north, became one of the jaws of a pincer movement that finally trapped Shozo's *28th Army* and sent it reeling back in defeat.

Further north, on the Imphal Plain, Lieutenant General Scoones IV Corps had, in accordance with Slim's wishes, been preparing for an attack of its own, Scoones pushing his three Indian divisions, the 17th, 20th and 23rd, steadily outwards, feeling for the enemy. During the course of these movements, skirmishes with enemy forces yielded documents and prisoners, which, combined with aerial reconnaissance reports and other sources of information, led Scoones and Slim to believe that a major Japanese attack was developing on the IV Corps front. Both Generals agreed that the best way to meet it would be to concentrate IV Corps on the relatively flat ground around Imphal where the Allied superiority in armoured units could be used to best effect. There were significant problems, however, and first among these was, as ever in Burma, the question of supply.

The Imphal Plain, a relatively flat area located in the mountainous region that separates the Brahmaputra Valley of India from the plains of central Burma, is some 40 miles (64km) long by 20 miles (32km) wide, and was at that time served by only one road worth the name, hacked out of the jungle from the railhead at Dimapur, 130 miles (209km) to the north, thence to wind its way southward past the hill station at Kohima and on to Imphal village itself, which lay at the northern end of the Plain. Along this single artery much of the food and equipment for IV Corps, and the many thousands of civilians working at the base, travelled. On the credit side, two vital all-weather airstrips had been constructed, one at Imphal village, and one at Palel, to the south.

General Slim was fully aware that the supply of IV Corps would be a significant problem, but a large part of his reasoning for fighting a defensive battle at Imphal was based on the fact that he would have his Japanese opponents themselves at the end of a long and potentially tenuous supply line. Attacking, as they would, with their usual tight logistical limits (Mutaguchi insisting to his subordinates that Imphal must be taken within three weeks[4]), Slim proposed keeping to his overall plan of denying Allied supplies to the enemy while using the Allied air forces not only to supply Imphal, but to harass and disrupt Mutaguchi's own greatly extended supply line.

Slims's planned 'coup de grace' at Imphal also relied heavily on the air forces. Once *15th Army* had been drawn onto the Plain and committed to an all-out attack, he proposed to replace 5 and 7 Divisions with troops from India and airlift them from the Arakan to Imphal to fight what he hoped might be the decisive struggle.

Mutaguchi's attack materialised at the end of March, and was pressed forward with all the fanatical bravery that was to be expected of the Japanese. The battle for Imphal and Kohima lasted until early June, and was, as the Iron Duke might have said, 'a damned close run thing', not least because the air forces were obliged not just to supply Imphal and airlift reinforcements, but supply 'Operation Thursday' Wingate's second, and much larger, Chindit operation, plus West African troops in the Kaladan Valley, Stillwell's divisions in the north of Burma, and maintain the airlift to China – all in the face of the determined efforts of the Japanese Army Air Force to thwart their efforts.[5]

In all his campaigns in India/Burma Slim had one focus – the absolute destruction of the enemy. The capture of territory was of no consequence by comparison. All along the vast Burma front, from the Chinese border in the north-east, through Imphal in Assam, to the Arakan in the south-west, in mid to late 1944 Japanese arms suffered significant setbacks, however they were far from being destroyed. Another great battle would be required to achieve that aim.

V

Lieutenant General Renya Mutaguchi led his *15th Army* to disastrous defeat at Imphal, Japanese war correspondents of the time talking of 'the greatest defeat in military history', with losses at the time estimated at not less than 53,000 men from a total of 85,000;[6] not that 'defeatism' such as this would ever see daylight in the newspapers of Japan. Elsewhere in Burma things also looked bleak for the Japanese. Shozo's *28th Army* barely escaped destruction in the Arakan, while in north eastern Burma Honda's *33rd Army* was hard pressed by both Stillwell's mainly Chinese Northern Combat Area Command (NCAC), and farther east still the Chinese XI and XX Army Groups, which had been pushing down from Yunnan Province since mid May.

In the face of these disasters, Lieutenant General Kawabe hurriedly sought to reorganise his Burma Area Army, drawing in reinforcements at a rate of 5,000 per month and making strenuous efforts to re-equip his battered divisions with guns, ammunition, and all the necessary paraphernalia of war. Following suspension of the Imphal attack on 4 July, Kawabe prepared a coordinated plan for his three armies:[7]

Operation Ban

15th Army to regroup along the line of the Zibyu Mountain Range through Mawlaik, Kalewa, and Gangaw, thereby short-ening their lines and gaining time for operations along the Irrawaddy.

Operation Kan

28th Army to prepare for defence of the coast bordering the Bay of Bengal against amphibious assault (a major re-invasion of Burma from the sea preoccupied the Japanese Command although it was never a real threat due to a lack of both landing craft and Allied warships to protect them from a powerful Japanese battle fleet based at Singapore).

Operation Dan

33rd Army to push the Chinese XI and XX Army Groups back into Yunnan, deny them access to the Burma Road and prevent a link up with Stillwell's NCAC.

The *33rd Army* fought desperately and had some success against the Chinese Yunnan Force. Honda deployed Lieutenant General Matsuyama's 11,000-strong *56th Division* along a line some 250 miles (402km) long, from the Hsipaw Pass south to Lashio, to face the twelve Chinese divisions of General Wei Li Huang, totalling approximately 72,000 men. Despite overwhelming numbers, the Chinese were bedevilled by significant problems in the shape of a long and tenuous line of communications and the inferior training of their infantry. These problems were not assisted when a Chinese transport aircraft in heavy cloud mistook a Japanese held airstrip at Tengechung for one of their own, and landed, delivering into captivity three Chinese staff officers bearing complete details of all Chinese formations taking part in the assault, and the new Chinese cipher. From then onwards Matsuyama had the singular privilege of having advance knowledge of his opponents movements and intentions. He used his advantage to good effect.

Inevitably, in the face of such a huge preponderance of numbers, *56th Division* was obliged to give ground, albeit slowly, and elsewhere on the *33rd Army* front a two and a half month battle for strategically significant Myitkyina ended when, on 3 August, Stillwell's NCAC finally captured the town and its vitally important airstrip. With Myitkyina in Allied hands the China airlift could swing south from Assam and so avoid the hazardous 'Hump' route across the Himalayas. It would also assist construction of the Ledo Road from Assam to Kunming.

Allied pressure continued without respite, *33rd Army* gradually withdrawing before the Chinese Yunnan force and the NCAC, and *15th Army* being pushed back towards the Chindwin by 14th Army.

VI

The Japanese suffered grievously in the latter half of 1944, but the problem of adequately supplying and feeding the men in this unforgiving terrain affected the Allies almost as badly, particularly since their supply lines lengthened as they went forward while those of the Japanese became correspondingly shorter.

14th Army advanced from Imphal into Burma with monsoon at its height and campaigning a nightmare of continual torrential rain and clinging, cloying, energy sapping, mud, mud, and more mud, which, despite the words of the old song, was not in the least bit glorious. The air forces continued their vital supply missions through this appalling weather, and while there were shortages from time to time, there was never a serious overall problem in getting enough to eat. There were, nevertheless, still significant problems in the areas of variation and quality of diet, with fresh meat and vegetables still chief among the deficiencies.

To the experienced eye of General Slim, the men, while cheerful enough now that they were advancing, were too thin, and he had his medical staff withdraw several British, Indian, and Gurkha battalions from the front line for rest and a thorough medical examination. The results were surprising as a great many of the men were found to be suffering from malnutrition, at that time also rife among the Japanese. In addition to the problems of quality of diet already referred to, 14th Army doctors reported that the continual strain of jungle fighting reacted on the metabolism of the men's bodies which passed food through without taking the normal amount of nourishment from it, with the inevitable adverse affect on their overall health. Over a twenty-six day period during July/ August, 9 Brigade, the lead unit of 5 Division advancing along the Tiddim Road, engaged in a number of hard-fought engagements, captured 18 prisoners, eleven tanks, fifteen field guns, nineteen mortars, thirty-three machine guns and over 200 lorries. During that same period the brigade suffered nine killed and eighty-five wounded, but lost 507 to sickness.[8] What could be done was done, but with refrigeration on the scale required a major problem, and continued campaigning an absolute necessity to deny the Japanese time to recover, the problems would persist.

VII

As soon as it became clear that the great battles around Imphal and Kohima would result in significant victory, Allied attention turned to the next phase of the campaign. During June the British Chiefs of Staff in London issued a directive in which they stated the objectives to be:

> To develop, broaden and protect the air link to China, in order to provide maximum and timely flow of petrol, oil, lubricants, and stores to China in support of Pacific operations. So far as is consistent with the above, to press advantages against the enemy by exerting maximum effort, ground and air, particularly during the current monsoon season, and in pressing such advantages to be prepared to exploit the development of overland communications to China. All these operations must be dictated by forces at present available or firmly allocated to SEAC.[9]

Two things stand out from this directive, the first being that it is weighted very much toward the American view of operations in Burma, and the second that SEAC could expect little more in terms of reinforcement.

It was plainly intended that any offensive operations would be undertaken in northern Burma with the express purpose of completing and opening the Ledo Road from Assam to China.[10] Elsewhere operations were to be largely of a 'holding' nature.

Such an approach did not suit Slim's offensive spirit, but he was not unduly dismayed as he believed that, even without further reinforcement, a full-blown invasion of Burma proper would be possible within the 'forces at present available' restriction, particularly as XXXIII Indian Corps joined 14th Army at Imphal and could combine with IV Corps for the main assault, while XV Corps remained in the Arakan to pin down *28th Army*.

On receipt of the directive from London, Staff at SEAC headquarters engaged in a flurry of planning and duly produced three distinct alternatives:

Plan X in which Stillwell's NCAC, reinforced by divisions from 14th Army, would be the main attack force and would secure north eastern Burma up to a line stretching from Katha, through Mongmit, to Lashio. At the same time the Yunnan Chinese were to push forward to achieve a link-up with NCAC at Lashio. 14th Army would conduct a limited offensive across the Chindwin.

Plan Y gave the main offensive role to 14th Army, which was to conduct a campaign to secure Mandalay and the surrounding area. The NCAC and Yunnan Chinese were to conduct an offensive from the north and link-up with 14th Army around Maymyo.

Plan Z proposed a combined amphibious/air operation to capture Rangoon, followed by a drive north to meet Allied forces coming from that direction.

Slim was convinced that a major operation to capture Mandalay was the way to proceed, but only as a stepping stone to an overland campaign aimed at the capture of Rangoon, and instructed his own staff to come up with an unofficial plan to that effect. What they produced was Operation Sea or Bust (SOB), which bore a striking similarity to Plan Y, but envisaged an onward drive down the valley of the Irrawaddy to Rangoon and the complete expulsion of the Japanese from Burma.

Mountbatten finally opted for elements of both Plans 'Y' and 'Z', to be known as Operation Capital and summarised as follows:

1. 14th Army to advance across the Chindwin, supported by 221 Group RAF, and occupy the area between that river and the Irrawaddy. The capture of Mandalay to be undertaken if practicable.
2. A simultaneous advance by NCAC and the Yunnan Chinese, supported by 10th and 14th USAAF, to a line from Thabbeikkyin through Mogok to Lashio.
3. A limited advance by XV Corps in the Arakan, supported by 224 Group RAF, to secure forward positions and prevent enemy action against Allied airfields.
4. As these operations progressed, the sea/air operation to capture Rangoon envisaged in Plan Z (codenamed 'Dracula'), to take place before the onset of monsoon 1945, i.e. not later than March of that year.

The Admiral's boundless enthusiasm and optimism can be seen in this ambitious plan, but General Slim doubted that it would ever come to fruition as it most certainly breached the 'forces at present available' stricture, notably with regard to the number of landing craft required for 'Dracula'. They were simply not available in South East Asia and would not be available until the fall of Germany, which, in mid 1944, seemed some way off.

At the end of July Slim discussed his concerns with General Giffard, C-in-C 11 Army Group. Giffard agreed that the 'Dracula' aspect of Mountbatten's plan was unlikely to be possible but issued orders for 14th Army to prepare for its part in 'Capital', to comprise a campaign in three phases:

1. The occupation, by land advance and an airborne operation, of the Kalewa-Kalemyo area.
2. An overland and airborne advance to secure the Shwebo plain.
3. The liberation of Burma as far south as the line Pakkoku–Mandalay, where 14th Army would make a junction with NCAC about Maymyo.

Given the almost complete lack of roads in the wild mountainous country to be encountered, Giffard assumed a significant amount of road building in the rear of the army as it advanced. Slim, however, maintained that the appreciable manpower requirement would be put to better use, and a more rapid advance maintained, if road building were to be kept within practicable limits, the airborne components of (1) and (2) in Giffard's plan cancelled, and the transport aircraft thus released used to keep 14th Army's forward elements supplied. Giffard agreed and Slim began preparations for the great offensive to commence in November, his intention being to bring the Japanese *15th Army* to battle once more, and hopefully this time to complete the work begun at Imphal. His preferred battleground would be the Shwebo plain, a large flat area between the Chindwin and Irrawaddy Rivers, north-west of Mandalay, and ideally suited to his advantage in armoured and mechanised units.

To assist implementation of the plan and allow Slim to concentrate all his efforts on the main Central Front, Giffard removed XV Corps and the Arakan front, plus the great line of communications to the rear, from commander 14th Army's responsibilities and placed them directly under HQ 11 Army Group.

During October a number of important Allied command changes took place. The prickly Stilwell, never easy to get on with, was removed from his various commands and sent home. An American triumvirate replaced him, Lieutenant General Dan Sultan taking command of NCAC, General A.C. Wedemeyer, Mountbatten's Deputy Chief of Staff, becoming adviser to Chiang Kai-shek, and General R.A. Wheeler taking over as Deputy Supreme Commander, SEAC.

Taking advantage of the reorganisation, Mountbatten took the opportunity to persuade the Combined Chiefs of Staff to replace a complicated, multi-layered command structure in the China/ Burma/India theatre, hurriedly put together bit by bit in response to intense Japanese pressure, with an Allied Land Forces commander and an integrated Anglo American Headquarters. Allied Land Forces South-East Asia (ALFSEA) replaced 11 Army Group and would have under command 14th Army, NCAC, XV Corps and Line of Communications Command. To Slim's regret General Giffard was not given the command but was replaced on 12 November by General Sir Oliver Leese, who had commanded XXX Corps in the Western Desert and subsequently, in Italy, succeeded General Montgomery in command of 8th Army, serving with some distinction, particularly during the battles for Monte Cassino and the assault on the Gothic Line.

Inevitably there were also command changes on the Japanese side of the hill. At the top, command of *Burma Area Army* passed from Kawabe to General Heitaro Kimura, while Mutaguchi, sent home in disgrace, was replaced as commander *15th Army* by Lieutenant General Katamura, promoted from command of *54th Division*. Lieutenant General Sakurai now commanded *28th Army* in the Arakan and Lieutenant General Honda retained command of *33rd Army*.

Chapter 2

The Long Road Back

I

General Slim fully expected Kimura, the new commander of *Burma Area Army*, to behave as other senior Japanese commanders and conduct a fanatical defence of every foot of ground between the Chindwin and the Irrawaddy. This would enable 14th Army to conduct, on the Shwebo plain, the type of European style battle for which it was best suited, with the accent on fast moving armoured and mechanised units backed by infantry. Kimura, however, did not oblige and had *15th Army* conduct an orderly retreat to the Irrawaddy, where, by January 1945, it was establishing itself in defensive positions along both banks, its area of responsibility from Singu in the north, southwards via Mandalay to a point between Myaungu and Chauk, where, nominally at least, the defences of *28th Army* were to begin. To the rear of *15th Army* lay the foothills of the Monglong Mountains, behind which arose the Shan Plateau.

Kimura was enough of a realist to appreciate that he could not defend all of Burma with the forces at his disposal, and seems to have had in mind something along the lines of an Imphal in reverse, namely bringing 14th Army to battle along the Irrawaddy where its supply lines, stretching from Assam over the 12,000 feet (3,657m) high Naga Hills, would be greatly extended and difficult to maintain. In this he gravely underestimated, as did virtually all Japanese commanders in Burma, both land and air, the critical significance of air supply.

In order to discuss his strategy for future operations and meet his senior officers face-to-face at this critical juncture, Kimura called a conference of his army commanders at Kalaw in early February. At that conference, in an appreciation that would prove to be highly perceptive, Lieutenant General Honda expressed the opinion that as his *33rd Army* had been obliged to contract its front to an area from

Lashio via Bawdin to Mongwit, as a consequence of which an Allied land route (the Ledo Road) from Assam to China had opened, the Chinese-American NCAC and the Yunnan Chinese would withdraw, neither the Americans or the Chinese having any interest in Burma beyond the establishment of a supply route into China, which had now been achieved. Any Chinese/US dispositions along these lines would leave 36 British Division virtually the only opposition in the north-eastern sector, in view of which, Honda believed, *Burma Area Army* should concentrate its forces for Operation Ban against its principal opponent, 14 Army around Mandalay.[11]

Kimura accepted the argument and, despite the fact that NCAC and the Yunnan Chinese still faced Honda's defences, withdrew *18th Division*, less one infantry regiment and one artillery battalion, from *33rd Army* and sent it to Mandalay to reinforce *15th Army*. Honda was to conduct a slow withdrawal in the north-east, while Kimura concentrated his forces for the proposed campaign along the Irrawaddy.[12]

Frustrated in his intention to complete the destruction of *15th Army* on the Shwebo plain, General Slim now faced a dilemma. The crossing of the Chindwin began in early December with XXXIII Corps (Lieutenant General Sir Montague Stopford) leading the way and IV Corps (now under the command of General Sir Frank Messervy) scheduled to follow and swing to the left of its predecessor. As the leading elements of XXXIII Corps approached the Irrawaddy a decision loomed as to where and when a crossing could best be made, and one thing at least was certain, against the fanatically determined opposition to be expected, wherever the attempt was made it would be no easy task.

From Male, north of Mandalay, south to Pakkoku and Pagan, the Irrawaddy wound its way for some 200 miles (322km). North of Mandalay its course lay through thick forest and jungle, and for the 24 miles (39km) between Thabeikkyin and Kyaumyaung, through a gorge 500 yards (457.2m) wide. Thereafter, between Myingyan and Pakkoku, generally the area of the confluence with the Chindwin, the surrounding country opened out, as did the width of the river, to a daunting 2,000–4,500 yards. During monsoon the current ran at about 5–6 mph, and in the dry season at around 2 mph along the wider stretches. Crossing would be considerably hampered by islands and sandbanks which changed position after each monsoon and therefore could not be accurately mapped, the difference in depth between maximum and minimum water levels was 31 feet (9.45m), in addition to which between March and April the river was subject to sudden rises. In general the eastern, or Japanese held, bank dominated 14th Army's approaches to the river, except in the area of the Sagaing Hills on the west bank in the Chindwdin/ Irrawaddy loop. These hills dominated approaches from the north, south, and east and were heavily fortified and defended by the Japanese.[13]

All in all, the river would be an extremely difficult obstacle to overcome by means of a straightforward frontal assault, and should 14th Army suffer serious reverses in the attempt, the advantage would soon pass to Kimura.

Slim and his staff had naturally considered alternatives to a battle on the Shwebo plain, and it was to one of these that the 14th Army commander now turned his attention. As originally conceived this plan called for XXXIII Corps to hold the Japanese at Mandalay while IV Corps marched south to Pakkoku, crossed the Irrawaddy at that point and marched north to take the Japanese in flank and rear. Bold and daring as it was, the plan had not previously been seriously considered for it was confidently assumed that Kimura would stand and fight west of the Irrawaddy, and 14th Army would need both corps conjoined for that one great battle. However, with Kimura's forces now fortified behind the Irrawaddy, General Slim decided to revive the Pakkoku flanking manoeuvre, but with modifications. XXXIII Corps would still pin the Japanese at Mandalay, making strenuous efforts to cross the river at various points in order to convince Kimura that this was the main assault, and oblige him to draw all his forces, including *Burma Area Army* reserve, *49th division* plus various other units currently in southern Burma, north for a decisive confrontation.

IV Corps, meanwhile, would have to make a long, tortuous flank march south to Pakkoku where it was to seize the crossing and send a powerful, fast, armoured spearhead, not north to attack Kimura's forces at Mandalay, but east to seize and hold Meiktila. The entire Corps would then fortify the town against the expected ferocious Japanese attempts at recapture.

14th Army formations to take part in the campaign would be:

IV Corps
7 and 17 Indian Divisions
255 Indian Tank Brigade (Sherman tanks)
Lushai Brigade
28 East African Brigade[14]

XXXIII Corps
2 British, 19 and 20 Indian Divisions
254 Indian Tank Brigade (Lee-Grant and Stuart tanks)
268 Brigade

II

Meiktila, together with Thazi, 12 miles farther east, held the key to
Kimura's position in northern Burma. Here were five located airfields and the chief supply bases for the Japanese *15th* and *33rd
Armies*, with all the attendant ammunition dumps, hospitals, and
depots that this entailed. Virtually all Japanese supplies, equipment,
and reinforcements came by ship to be unloaded at Rangoon, from
where such road and rail links that led to the combat areas came
together at Meiktila before pushing on north 'like', as Slim suc-
cinctly put it, 'the extended fingers of a hand, whose wrist was
Meiktila. Crush that wrist, no blood would flow to the fingers, the
whole hand would be paralysed ...'.[15]

Serious consideration had been given to the possibility of making
the assault on Meiktila an all-airborne operation, but trained parachute troops were in short supply and in any event the airlift
capability allotted to 14th Army by Eastern Air Command (EAC)
would barely suffice for supply missions and little more. Despite
the problems involved, it was as well that Meiktila finally became
allotted to IV Corps, for, as a harbinger of things to come, dawn of
10 December saw General Slim awoken to the unexpected sound
of numbers of aircraft taking off and passing low over his headquarters at Imphal. Japanese forces in China had launched a major
attack, and, without forewarning, three USAAF transport squadrons, seventy-five aircraft in total, were withdrawn from maintenance of 14th Army and despatched to China to bolster support
for the hard pressed Chinese army.

Staff officers rarely come in for much in the way of praise, however crises such as the one now facing 14th Army, for crisis it most certainly was, spotlight the essential nature of their work in making any operation successful. The loss of the three squadrons threatened to bring Slim's operations to a halt, yet he was determined to press on and the staff at Army, IV Corps, and XXXIII Corps headquarters, in combination with their opposite numbers at EAC, were obliged, in double-quick time, to completely re-calculate and re-plan the entire airlift operation, which they did, successfully. Inevitably someone had to suffer and that turned out to be XV Corps in the Arakan, which had its airlift significantly reduced to help make up the deficit.

For their part Eastern Air Command did what they could to make up the shortfall. Nos 117 and 194 Squadrons RAF, not long withdrawn for rest and retraining, were hurriedly returned to service and in late December Nos 435 and 436 Squadrons RCAF arrived in theatre to be allocated to 14th Army.

It should also be borne in mind that, while strenuous efforts were being made to make up the shortfall, the aircrew and ground crew of those squadrons still allocated to 14th Army were obliged to cram yet more flights into an already hectic schedule in an effort to keep supply build-up for the coming campaign at a manageable level; and yet, despite superhuman efforts on the part of those involved, the timetable for the operation slipped back, probably by some two to three weeks, at a time when giving the Japanese as much as a day more than necessary in which to rest and refit was regarded with great concern. Directly connected to this matter of not allowing Kimura time, there loomed a problem of immense significance in the form of the impending monsoon, due to start in April.

In January 1945, Admiral Mountbatten received new instructions from the Combined Chiefs of Staff instructing him that he was to go all-out for a rapid liberation of Burma as a prelude to the re-taking of Malaya and the opening of the Straits of Malacca. As Slim had always wanted, and indeed planned for, this allowed him to make a rapid thrust for Rangoon once Meiktila was securely in 14th Army hands. It also imposed a very tight schedule, for Rangoon must be taken before the onset of monsoon in order that large scale supply and reinforcement could arrive by sea at that port. Should Rangoon not fall in time, and those facilities not be available, EAC would face the unenviable task of attempting to keep upwards of 300,000 men supplied through some of the most atrocious weather conditions to be experienced in any theatre of war, 14th Army's advance would slow to a crawl and Kimura might be granted months until the monsoon blew itself out in which to regroup.

A rider to the Combined Chiefs of Staff directive reiterated the US position as regards their objectives in China/Burma/India and the use of US resources in that theatre. It bears repeating as it would have some impact on the campaign to come:

- The primary military object of the United States in the China and India-Burma theatres is the continuance of aid to China on a scale that will permit the full co-utilisation of the area and resources of China for operations against the Japanese. United States resources are deployed in India-Burma to provide direct or indirect support for China. Present forces and resources participate not only in operating the bases and lines of communication for United States and Chinese forces in China, but also constitute a reserve immediately available to China without permanently increasing the requirements of transport supplies to China.

- The United States Joint Chiefs of Staff contemplate no change in their agreement to Supreme Allied Commander South East Asia's (SACSEA) use of resources of the United States India-Burma theatre in Burma when this use does not prevent the fulfilment of their primary object of rendering support to China including protection of the lines of communication. Any transfer of forces engaged in approved operations in progress in Burma which is contemplated by the United States Joint Chiefs of Staff and which in the opinion of the British Chiefs of Staff would jeopardise these operations will be subject to discussion by the Combined Chiefs of Staff.[16]

III

With IV Corps crossing the Chindwin in the area of Tamu and beginning to move north, their direction of march would need a rapid change to the southward for a 328 mile (528km) march to Pakkoku. At the great battles of the 'Admin Box', Imphal, and Kohima, General Slim used weaknesses in Japanese logistical and administrative planning to inflict crushing defeats upon them, however the flanking move now being put into operation threatened to put 14th Army in exactly the same vulnerable position. The rough dirt road that IV Corps was to use (for most of the distance there was just one road) raised clouds of chocking dust in dry weather, and sucked vehicles down to their axles in mud in wet. Over this road was required to pass an entire corps – infantry, transport, tanks, guns and animals – plus a build up of supplies and ammunition to launch an opposed river crossing at the end of the march, plus fuel for the dash to Meiktila. All within two months and in complete secrecy. If Kimura discovered that Slim's two corps were widely separated he would be presented with a golden opportunity to defeat both in detail.

The IV Corps line of march would of necessity stretch for mile upon mile. Much of the column would need to be supplied by air transport, for which airstrips capable of accommodating transport aircraft and their fighter escorts would require construction as the corps advanced. A mammoth undertaking, but air supply would help to alleviate the vexed question of fresh meat and vegetables, for the lead units of the Corps at least. Rear elements would be supplied by road, the one existing road being rebuilt to an acceptable standard as the troops advanced. To assist with roadbuilding Major General W.F. Hasted, Slim's Chief Engineer, adopted the use of 'bithes', overlapping strips of Hessian cloth dipped in bitumen, for a quickly laid water-resistant surface (an idea quite possibly borrowed from the air forces, who had been using a similar method for the rapid construction of all-weather airstrips for some time). The road underneath the 'bithes' needed to be flattened, packed tight, with deep ditches constructed on either side fed by numerous run-off areas to keep torrential rain off the surface. The almost total lack of any road building equipment ensured that this was all back-breaking manual labour, but it worked, and at the height of the campaign 100 miles of this road carried 1,000 trucks per day in all weathers.

Victory or defeat was largely a question of supply for the voracious mechanised armies of the industrialised nations, and in addition to air and road, a more traditional method of transport in this mountainous jungle-clad country was also pressed into service by 14th Army – its rivers. By early 1945 most of the existing river craft on the Chindwin and the Irrawaddy had been destroyed, by British forces during the retreat of 1942, and since then by the Allied air forces that remorselessly strafed and bombed anything that might remotely be of use to the Japanese. At the beginning of the advance in January 1945 Major General Hasted was instructed by Slim that from a standing start, with practically nothing available that would float, he expected 500 tons of supplies to be moving down the Chindwin to the Irrawaddy within two months. The one thing Hasted did have was plenty of timber and in the space of weeks his own engineers, backed by construction companies from India and local Burmese labour, were turning out dumb barges in number. Ungainly and unsophisticated they certainly were, but three lashed together would load anything up to a Sherman tank.

Powered boats were a problem and would remain so, but outboard engines, marine petrol engines, and even a few small tugs (in kit form and requiring assembly on the riverbank) were flown in. As the military and civilian engineers got into their stride they even managed to salvage a number of useful craft, including a steamer or two, from the river bottom, using equipment improvised on the spot.

The main 'shipyard' was at Kalewa on the Chindwin, and perhaps their most unusual job was the construction, on Slim's orders, of a couple of small steam powered 'gunboats' armed with a Bofors gun, two Oerlikons and two Browning light automatics. These diminutive craft hoisted the white ensign and were manned by Royal Navy crewmen 'landlocked' with the ground forces since fall of Rangoon in 1942. The two boats saw a lot of action, and according to Slim 'maintained the real Nelsonian tradition of steering closer to the enemy'.[17]

The convoluted ground-based supply route that 14th Army would need illustrates just how important air transport would come to be:

- From the railhead at Dimapur in Assam, all-weather road via Imphal to Tamu – 206 miles (331km).
- A fair-weather road (which with the use of 'bithes' etc. might be brought up to all-weather status) to Kalewa – 112 miles (180km).

- Across the Chindwin by Bailey bridge, fair-weather road to Shwebo, then by a very bad, but all-weather, road to Mandalay and XXXIII Corps – 190 miles (306km).
- Onward to IV Corps by river link from Kalewa on the Chindwin to Myingyan on the Irrawaddy – 200 miles (322km).
- Myingyan to Meiktila partially by all-weather road and partially by rail (if the railway could be repaired and locomotives obtained) – 59 miles (95km).

Given that the airlift would be of crucial importance it should be kept in mind that while, for instance, the Douglas C47 'Dakota' had a range of 2,125 miles (3,420km), the farther away from the main air bases at Imphal and Chittagong that the ground forces drew, the faster the load carried and the rate of turn-around deteriorated until, beyond 250 miles (402km), the lift began to become impractical.[18] As a consequence great importance was placed on any XV Corps operations in the Arakan which would lead to the prompt capture of the islands of Akyab and Ramree, with their vital airfields (see map on p. xvi).

For some time 81st West African Division had been pushing southward down the Kaladan Valley, obliging their Japanese opposition to withdraw troops from Akyab to meet the threat, until, by the end of December, XV Corps intelligence reported that not much more than one battalion remained of the garrison. An assault force comprising 3 Commando Brigade, backed by 224 Group and a naval bombardment squadron, were primed and ready to go. However, on 2 January, an air observation post artillery officer, circling Akyab in a light aircraft, saw no Japanese in view and landed on an airstrip in the centre of the island. It transpired that the last defenders had been withdrawn forty-eight hours previously and the island was taken without the anticipated battle, although the town and all important airstrips were heavily damaged, both by Allied bombing and Japanese demolition.

Ramree Island was doubly important for it not only contained another vital airfield, on its north-western tip at Kyaukpyu, but an anchorage, also at Kyaukpyu, capable of accepting ocean going merchantmen. Capture of the island would therefore enable supplies to be transported in large quantity by sea from India and flown to 14th Army, removing considerable strain from the tortuous land/ river route already referred to.

Ramree had not been abandoned by the Japanese and it was reported that they were placing guns in caves covering proposed landing beaches along the north-west coast of the island. A brigade of 26 Indian Division was selected for the attack, and heavy air strikes backed by naval bombardment, which included the battle-ship *Queen Elizabeth*, prepared the way. The amphibious assault went in 21 January and Kyaukpyu was soon in Allied hands. Ground forces continued operations against the remaining Japanese, while repair and reconstruction of both anchorage and airfield began immediately.

There remained the contentious question of the number of transport aircraft available. Since the unexpected withdrawal of the three US squadrons in December the allocation to 14th Army had simply not been enough, a backlog of supplies was building up awaiting transportation, and the advance slowing in consequence.

During early January Generals Leese and Stratemeyer (Air Officer Commanding, EAC), made representations to Mountbatten calculating that at least 100 extra transport aircraft would be required by 1 February for military use, plus an extra forty to supply the civilian population in liberated areas. Interestingly, Combat Cargo Task Force (CCTF), the joint Anglo-American air transport grouping which actually flew the vast amounts of supply and equipment to the ground forces, disagreed. CCTF believed that the need was for more efficient use of the aircraft then available, and in particular the forward preparation of a number of large supply dumps with attendant airstrips, which would in large measure offset the 250-mile effective range restriction. The islands of Akyab and Ramree were earmarked for just such a role but it would take time to get them into operation.

Both approaches had their strengths and weaknesses but Mount-batten opted to try for more aircraft as potentially the quickest solution to the problem, and telegraphed an appreciation to the Chiefs of Staff in London. Such was the critical nature of the difficulty faced that he also decided to despatch his own new Chief of Staff, Lieutenant General F.A.M. Browning,[19] home to press the case. Despite being advised by London that Browning's trip would not be necessary, Mountbatten sent him anyway with instructions to underline the fact that the extra aircraft represented literally the success or failure of the current campaign.

Browning's mission was a success and resulted in Supreme Allied Commander, Mediterranean, Field-Marshall Sir Harold Alexander (himself no stranger to Burma, having been GOC there during the dark days of 1942), sending one RAF squadron of twenty-five Dakotas, and First Sea Lord, Admiral of the Fleet Sir Andrew Cunningham, sending on loan a squadron of thirty similar aircraft that had been earmarked for Australia in support of the recently formed British Pacific Fleet. Finally, representations in Washington succeeded in persuading the US Administration to request Lieutenant General Wedemeyer (Chief of Staff to Chiang Kai-shek) to return by 1 February two of the USAAF squadrons withdrawn in December. In addition, the eight RAF transport squadrons at that time operated by SEAC were to be strengthened from twenty-five to thirty aircraft. The net result was an improvement in the shape of 145 aircraft – five more than actually requested – but it would not be the last time that this particular problem would rear its head.

IV

The new aircraft could not arrive too soon. On XXXIII Corps front air supply had been reduced to the maintenance of only three brigades, the balance of Corps supply coming via the precarious road from Dimapur, a journey of some 400 miles (644km) by mid January. In order to relieve to some extent the drain on manpower entailed in defending this extended line of communication, Lieutenant General Stopford formed for the purpose a mobile Corps reserve comprising 268 Indian Infantry Brigade and elements of 254 Indian Tank Brigade. This reduced the depletion of forward operational detachments and enabled the advance to continue relatively unhindered by Japanese raids to cut in the land supply line. Nevertheless, he was still obliged to slow his advance until the increased air element became operational.

Despite supply problems two brigades of 19 Indian Division fought their way eastwards to arrive at the Irrawaddy along the line of the 24 mile (39km) long gorge north of Mandalay. Reconnaissance crossings over the defile were soon made, followed by a major crossing to establish a bridgehead at Thabeikkyin on 14 January, and at Kyaukmyaung the following day. Evidently taken by surprise, the Japanese did not react until the division was well established on the eastern bank, but when the counter attacks came they were fierce and determined. 19 Indian Division held, assisted by 36 British Division of Lieutenant General Sultan's NCAC. 36 Division established contact with the 19th mid December and five days before Christmas crossed to the eastern bank of the Irrawaddy at Katha, to the north of Thabeikkyin, and was pushing south toward the 19 Indian bridgehead.

These vigorous crossings, plus deception measures used to indicate that the 19th was backed by two more (in fact non-existent) divisions, helped convince Kimura that 14th Army would make its main attempt to cross the Irrawaddy north of Mandalay. This was entirely intentional and designed by Slim to ensure that his opposite number drew most of his available force, from all over Burma, as far north as possible. Slim would then make his main XXXIII Corps crossing south of Mandalay, and spring the trap shut with the IV Corps assault on Meiktila.

As part of the deception to convince Kimura that he faced all of 14th Army around Mandalay, a fake IV Corps Headquarters, using the same wireless channels hitherto used by the real HQ, was established at Tamu and continued radio traffic as if the Corps remained on the Shwebo plain.

The actual IV Corps, meanwhile, had begun its advance south toward Pakkoku, and was obliged to maintain strict radio silence with the exception of a minimal amount of disguised traffic through 28 East African Brigade, in the van of the advance together with the Lushai Brigade. It being impossible to completely shield the fact that some Allied units were on the move southward, 28 East African Brigade operated under the guise of 11 East African Division, with instructions to give the the Japanese the impression by means of radio traffic etc. that their objective was the oilfields at Yenangyaung.

The first serious opposition to be encountered by IV Corps was at the town of Gangaw, where the Lushai Brigade bumped into well entrenched Japanese infantry. Lieutenant General Messervy had a frustrating problem in that he commanded overwhelming numbers in the shape of a full corps, but could not use them as this would undoubtedly give the lie to the deception and warn Kimura of the flanking movement. Restricted to using only the Lushai Brigade and the East Africans as ground assault forces, he called on EAC to launch an air attack. Mitchell medium bombers duly bombed the area, followed by fighters strafing the defenders to keep their heads down while the Allied infantry went in. After two days of heavy fighting the East Africans and the Lushai Brigade cleared Gangaw, and organised Japanese resistance in the valley was over.

By January 1945 the once fearsome Japanese Army Air Force was a much reduced adversary in Burma but they still had a few of the fast, high flying Mitsubishi Ki-46 'Dinah' reconnaissance aircraft available, and 221 Group fighters were obliged to pay particular attention to keeping these and any other enemy aircraft well away from the IV Corps line of march, for in the dry pre-monsoon weather a line of thick red dust thrown up by Corps vehicles could be seen for miles from the air.

It was around the time of the Gangaw battle that Lieutenant General Messervy began to be concerned as to just how long the deception measures in place might fool the Japanese. Following Gangaw 7 Indian Division took over at the head of the column, 28 East African and the Lushai Brigade swinging further south to increase the impression of an attack on Yenangyaung.

The intention was for 7 Indian Division to force a crossing of the Irrawaddy in the Pakkoku – Pagan area and for 255 Indian Tank Brigade to pass through the bridgehead and make a dash for Meiktila, capturing Thabutkon airfield on the way so that reinforcements might be flown in. It was realised, however, that a tank brigade alone could not take and hold Meiktila for any length of time against determined counter-attack and would need rapid reinforcement. General Messervy therefore recommended that his second division, 17 Indian, be put on an entirely mechanised and air transportable footing. General Slim agreed and the division was brought from Dimapur to Imphal where the change was made, both 11 East African Division, which had been withdrawn from the front, and 5 Indian Division, in Army reserve, being stripped of most of their vehicles in order to make the change. In this way two brigades of 17 Indian Division became fully mechanised in double-quick time while the third, 99 Brigade, was made fully air transportable. This entailed all the brigade vehicles, including its 25-pounder guns, being fitted with narrow 'Jury' axles to enable them to be wheeled onto and out of Dakota transports. The two mechanised brigades

were then moved rapidly into forward concentration (an administrative nightmare in itself) ready for a rapid advance in support of
255 Indian Tank Brigade.

7 Indian Division now approached the Irrawaddy, its first task to
clear the Pauk area and enable construction of an airstrip capable of
taking transport aircraft. Airfield construction was an ongoing
feature of the campaign, and a headache for the engineers due to the
dry, crumbly nature of the soil, with its propensity to break up and
form a layer of dust that could easily be as much as 2 feet deep.
Japanese airstrips were taken over and repaired where possible, but,
dependant upon how much warning they had been given, Japanese
counter measures could cause significant delays. As an example, on
at least one occasion an airstrip was found have been completely
covered by nine inches of hand-packed stone.

From Pauk 7 Division made its way over the difficult Pondaung
Range, the aforementioned dust causing considerable problems, and
from there Messervy sent patrols surreptitiously forward to scout
for suitable crossing places. Having considered all the alternatives
he chose Nyaungu, the Irrawaddy here being at its narrowest in
his front, but at 1,000 yards (914m) wide, still a substantial obstacle,
not least due to a shortage of boats, particularly powered craft. A
battalion or two of parachute troops would have greatly simplified
the problem, but, as with much else, they were simply not available.

To keep the Japanese guessing, Messervy planned several diversionary demonstrations in addition to the main assault. These were
to be at Pakkoku and Pagan, plus a crossing by 28 East African
Brigade at Chauk. All the proposed crossings, Nyaungu and the
deceptions, were meticulously planned since, with the vagaries of
war in mind, there were no certainties as to which one, if any, might
succeed.

Photographic reconnaissance missions were flown along the
Irrawaddy on a daily basis and from this and other sources (captured documents, radio intercepts etc.) it was established that on
the 7 Division front, Kimura still had no idea of the storm that
was about to break on his line of communications, his troops remaining disposed thinly along the river. *2nd Indian National Army
Division*[20], variously estimated at between 5,000 and 10,000 strong,
backed by four battalions of the Japanese *72 Independent Mobile
Brigade*, covered a long stretch of the river from Chauk to Nyaungu,

while *214 Regiment* held the area of Pakkoku. One further advantage accrued to the crossing at Nyaungu in that *72 Independent Mobile Brigade* formed the extreme right of *28th Army*, while *214 Brigade* formed the extreme left of *15th Army*. The two units therefore operated under completely different chains of command and valuable time would be lost coordinating their response.

With Japanese forces still very much in evidence on the west bank of the Irrawaddy, the leading elements of 7 Division fought their way toward the crossing areas. 114 Brigade encountered a strong enemy detachment from *3rd battalion 214 Brigade* well dug-in on high ground at the Kanhla crossroads 8 miles from Pakkoku, and it was 10 February before the brigade, supported by tanks, dislodged these stubborn defenders. 89 Brigade arrived opposite Pagan, the ancient capital of Burma, and by night despatched a Sikh patrol across the river. The patrol remained hidden on the east bank and reported by radio that the southern end of the town appeared unoccupied. In view of the apparent weakness of the defences at Pagan, Major General G.C. Evans, Officer Commanding 7 Division, decided to upgrade the 'feint' at that point to a full-blown assault.

South of Pagan 28 East African Brigade overcame stiff resistance to gain its objective, Seikpyu, and put in train preparations for its crossing, while to the north 33 Brigade, which was to make the main assault at Nyaungu, occupied Myitche on the west bank and also made its preparations.

Chapter 3

One More River to Cross

I

Across the Irrawaddy from Mandalay a mobile column comprising 4, 5, and 6 Brigades of 2 British Division thrust southward to seize the main XXXIII Corps crossing points in the Myinmu area (see map on p. xii), where the river curved westward after passing Mandalay before resuming its southward course to Myingyan. 5 Brigade reached the Irrawaddy and cleared much of the bank of enemy occupation in the Mu River/Myittha area although stubborn resistance continued at Ywathitgyi.

Air strikes were called in and on 31 January Ywathitgyi was subjected to fierce pounding by B25s, Thunderbolts and Hurribombers, following which units of 5 Brigade occupied the eastern end of the town. However, using stone buildings to great effect, Japanese defence continued until, on 2 February, further air strikes were called in and that same evening 1 Royal Scots finally overcame any remaining opposition. Meanwhile, on 28 January, 4 Brigade attacked Kyaukse and, supported by the ubiquitous Hurribombers and Thunderbolts of 221 Group, captured the town on 4 February.

6 Brigade now moved forward to the Yawathitgyi area and, with 5 Brigade, made preparations for the crossing, while 4 Brigade moved on to Sagaing to prevent interference from Japanese forces established there.

Crossings and threats of crossings to the north and south of Mandalay greatly occupied the attention of General Kimura, and in early February he came to the conclusion that the main threat from 14th Army was not after all to the north of Mandalay, but in the 2 Division area around Myinmu as the British division was known to be supported by an additional force (20 Indian Division) advancing on its right. Accordingly Kimura switched artillery and other elements of *15th* and *53rd Divisions* from containment of the

19 Indian Division bridgeheads north of Mandalay, to the vicinity of Ngazun, opposite Myinmu.[21] He remained blissfully unaware of the IV Corps threat to the Pagan and Pakkoku crossing points and continued to draw much of his available force to the Mandalay area. In fact, so unconcerned were the Japanese that in early February Field Marshal Count Terauchi, Supreme Commander, Kimura's superior and Mountbatten's opposite number, ordered the withdrawal of *2nd Division* from Pakkoku and despatched it to what was then French Indo-China (now Vietnam).

It was planned that a major crossing would be made by 20 Indian Division at Myinmu during the night of 12/13 February to keep Kimura's attention away from IV Corps, which would begin its advance at Pakkoku concurrently. Major General Gracey, Officer Commanding 20 Division, put in place several diversionary feints and planned for two actual crossings, the principal attempt by 100 Indian Infantry Brigade at Myinmu, and a subsidiary assault by 32 Indian Infantry Brigade in the Cheyadaw area 7 miles downstream. To established the level of opposition that might be encountered, the days leading up to the 20 Division assault were used to put numerous patrols across the river, backed by aerial reconnaissance. It emerged from these efforts that a light screen of Japanese infantry was in place along the opposite bank, supported by heavier concentrations farther back disposed in a semi-circle ready to pounce on any landing attempt. A reasonable estimate of the strength of defensive artillery was possible from the shelling of 20 Division positions that took place.

The Japanese artillery was located in two main concentrations and was subjected to numerous attacks from the air, culminating on the afternoon of 12 February with a major raid comprising fifty Liberator heavy bombers, plus a squadron of Lightnings dropping napalm. This caused the destruction of a number of guns and the dispersal of those remaining, relieving the assault forces of the necessity to face concentrated artillery fire until the guns could be regrouped.

The immediate objective of the 20 Division crossing was for 100 and 32 Infantry Brigades to establish linked bridgeheads and pass 80 Indian Infantry Brigade through to cut the Meiktila–Mandalay road, thereby severing one of the principal arteries linking Kimura's forces.

The Irrawaddy at this point was some 1,500 yards (1,372m) wide and obstructed by partially submerged sandbanks. The river ran in strong currents between these sandbanks and a number of heavily laden boats from 2 Border Regiment,[22] the 100 Brigade spearhead, were swept downstream. Difficulties were compounded by the fact that a high wind blew and it was not possible to warm up outboard motors prior to the attempt due to the resultant noise.

To assist the assault the Beach Reconnaissance Unit crossed prior to 2 Border, and swimmers from the Sea Recce Unit fixed guiding lights on the far bank. The defence was slow to react and initially consisted of light machine gun fire, the Japanese evidently believing that this was just more patrol activity. Consequently, with the coming of daylight the whole of 2 Border was established across the river and had been joined by 14 Frontier Force Rifles and one company of 4/10 Gurkha Rifles. By 0900 hours on the 13th a number of anti-tank guns and mortars were across, as were two bulldozers and several jeeps.

One reason for the slowness of the Japanese response was the success of the 32 Brigade diversionary assault downstream which, as planned, drew Japanese forces away from Myinmu; however by the 14th the defence had recovered and the 100 Brigade bridgehead was subjected to mortar fire and counter attack.

Among the Japanese opposing the 100 Brigade crossing was Second Lieutenant Kazuo Imai, *12th Company, 3rd Battalion, 215 Infantry Regiment, 33 Division, 15 Army*, who, on the night of 15 February was part of a detachment that included the *Yokoyama Machine Gun Platoon* sent to disrupt the landings in support of an artillery bombardment. Under the command of Lieutenant Midorikawa, Imai and the detachment crawled toward their objective along a narrow sandy beach with the river to their left, awaiting the opening of the artillery barrage that would be their signal to attack.

The sounds of generators and outboard motors were clearly audible from the bridgehead as Imai lay in the sand, and lights that he took to be signal lamps flashed back and forth across the river. Warily Imai stood up and drew his sword, making his way stealthily toward what he believed to be the edge of the enemy position. As he did so Japanese artillery opened fire, their shells falling short of the target onto the plateau above the landing beach.

This both surprised and concerned Imai as, not only was the barrage inaccurate, it had begun too early.

Suddenly an enemy soldier rose up out of the darkness a little way ahead of him and Imai charged forward, raised his sword above his head and swung it down. The Japanese felt the blade strike home and heard the soldier 'roar', while simultaneously detonating a grenade. Imai was blown backwards and lay flat in the sand, wounded in both legs by the explosion.

Flares lit up the area and somebody called 'enemy in the river'. Glancing to his left the wounded Second Lieutenant called for an accompanying light machine gun to open fire on several boats moving toward the *12th Company* position from upstream. The gun jammed and Imai ordered that it be disassembled and cleaned. Mortar shells fell on the beach and Lieutenant Yokoyama set up a medium machine gun to Imai's right. The gun opened fire and the wounded Japanese was obliged to experience the highly unpleasant sensation of having 'friendly' fire pass closely over his prone form as the gun engaged the boats.

The machine gun switched its aim from the boats to the plateau and enemy tracer criss-crossed the area in response. Unit commander Midorikawa arrived and, although wounded himself, took up Imai's sword with the intention of leading a charge. With the beach still peppered by mortar fire Imai attempted to cushion himself from the explosions, until, with some slackening of the fire, he looked up but could no longer see Midorikawa. Bullets from Yokoyama's machine gun were now spattering the sand close to his feet and Imai saw that the gunner was dead, his finger still pressing the trigger. A shadowy figure pushed the dead gunner aside and took his place. He too was killed and replaced by a third gunner who continued firing until his ammunition ran out. Shortly thereafter Imai was rendered unconscious by an explosion.

Regaining his senses some time later the Second Lieutenant discovered the beach returned once more to relative dark and quiet, and by slipping silently into the river managed to return to company headquarters where he discovered that Midorikawa had also survived. In this sharp, bloody little fight, representative of so many more actions, large and small, taking place up and down the river, *12th Company* lost fourteen men killed or missing, and the Machine Gun Company nine.[23]

II

On the IV Corps front in the area surrounding Pagan, the vital crossings, the crux of the entire campaign, were scheduled for the night of 13/14 February. Continuing with thus far successful deception measures to the last minute, farther south 28 East African Brigade was to make a demonstration against the oil town of Chauk, to reinforce the impression that all this activity was the prelude to an assault on the Yenangyaung oilfields.

To facilitate close ground/air cooperation the headquarters of both 14th Army and 221 Group were established alongside each other at Imphal, moving forward jointly to Monywa during early February, the Monywa HQ being situated partly in the jungle and partly in some of the less battle scarred buildings. Departing Japanese liberally 'salted' the area with booby traps, but Slim's main concern centred on the snakes that frequented the area, and seemed particularly drawn to the vicinity of the War Room, selected as, despite being devoid of a roof, it had a good solid concrete floor. The General made it a practice to visit the War Room on a nightly basis to check the latest situation maps before retiring to bed, and on one such occasion he narrowly avoided stepping on a krait, a small but deadly snake. Slim thereafter took to using a torch, an action calculated to furrow the brows of his security officers since it could well draw the attention of snipers, Japanese artillery fire or snooping aircraft – any or all of which he considered less likely than snake bite![24]

With the IV Corps advance the area of operations covered by 221 Group grew to a front of over 200 miles in length by approximately the same in depth, and was destined to grow much larger as the months progressed. All aircraft engaged in close (as opposed to tactical) support of 14th Army were controlled by HQ 221 Group, however, for the crucial period now about to commence exceptions were made as extra air cover was drafted in to cover the vital assault on Meiktila. Two USAAF Air Commando Groups were operated directly from HQ Eastern Air Command, while the Mustang squadrons of Second Air Commando, USAAF, were operated from the advanced HQ of Combat Cargo Task Force as it moved forward in tandem with Messervy's HQ IV Corps. Additional air cover was provided by the four Thunderbolt squadrons of 903 Wing, RAF, which, being based in the Arakan, remained under 224 Group.

Principal 221 Group units allocated to IV Corps were 152 Squadron RAF (Spitfires), 11 Squadron RAF (Hurribombers) and 1 Squadron Indian Air Force (Hurricanes – Tactical Reconnaissance).

Selected to make the main crossing at Nyaungu, 33 Indian Infantry Brigade engaged in training exercises with divisional engineers at Gangaw – and they would need all the preparation they could get for the task facing the brigade was not an easy one. Soon after their arrival along the Irrawaddy an inspection of the river disclosed that the level had dropped, revealing new sandbanks which meant that the shortest route – straight across – would not be practicable and that an oblique approach would be necessary. After dark units of the Special Boat Service assisted by frogmen would take soundings and chart routes, the final courses selected varying from 1,500 yards (1372m) to over 2,000 yards (1829m), this last being the longest opposed river crossing undertaken anywhere during the Second World War.

Topography also posed a significant problem as the west bank, occupied by 7 Division, was largely cultivated with rice fields so low lying as to be almost at river level, while the east bank rose to a height of some 102 feet (30m) intersected by dry chaungs (river beds) every few hundred yards. Aerial reconnaissance revealed Japanese positions scattered along the opposing bluffs, but in the days leading up to the assault did not show any great intensifying of defensive preparations in the areas facing 33 Brigade, with the exception of new works which appeared just east of Nyaungu. A certain amount of additional defensive digging was noted, however, opposite areas where vigorous feints were in operation (28 East African Brigade south of Pagan, and 114 Indian Infantry Brigade to the north around Pakkoku).

To take maximum advantage of surprise the original intention was to make a rapid crossing in daylight soon after 33 Brigade arrived, with heavy air, artillery, and tank support to quash defensive positions, but a shortage of transport aircraft underscored by inevitable delays with the tortuous land supply line decreed that insufficient ammunition would be available in time. A completely silent night crossing was then considered, but as there would be no moon it was felt that asking boats to negotiate serpentine indirect channels in complete darkness would invite disaster.

Finally a plan in four phases was devised to begin just before dawn, comprising:

1. An assault crossing, the first flight of which was to be silent and at night, launched from points on the west bank, and a ½ to 3 miles upstream of Nyaungu, to seize four beaches and the cliffs 1 mile north-east of the village on the east bank. For the assault crossing the South Lancashire Regiment was taken on loan from 114 Indian Infantry Brigade as they had experience in boat work and had taken part in the landing at Madagascar.
2. A rapid follow-up in daylight of the three battalions of 33 Brigade and some tanks, under all available covering fire, to build up the bridgehead.
3. A rapid advance from the bridgehead to capture Nyaungu and with it the eastern end of the shortest river crossing, which would be organised and put into operation at once.
4. Expansion of the bridgehead to take 17 Indian Division which would cross as soon as possible by the direct Nyaungu route.[25]

Even if the landings went without a hitch it was unlikely that the full brigade would be across the Irrawaddy in less than seven hours.

Intelligence from, amongst other sources, the Sikh patrol from 89 Brigade across the river in the Pagan area, indicated Pagan to Nyaungu to be occupied by the Nehru Brigade of the INA, approximately 700–1,000 strong, leavened by two companies of Japanese infantry.[26] This was encouraging news as less resistance might be expected from the INA than the fanatical Japanese, however time was very short and as divisional engineers could not in daylight move up the hardware for their appointed tasks, including heavy, cumbersome items such as bridging equipment on transporter lorries, further time was lost bringing these heavy loads over sandy uneven tracks in complete darkness. The engineers were then obliged to disguise all signs of movement from prying eyes on the bluffs opposite before dawn streaked the eastern sky .

Nevertheless, by the morning of 13 February all troops and equipment were concealed within easy reach of the crossing points. Downstream 28 East African Brigade were making a strong demonstration against Chauk, while upstream 114 Indian Infantry Brigade had captured Pakkoku, forcing the Japanese to reinforce the area and occupy an island in the river to oppose any possible crossing at that point. Both flank diversions successfully drew defending infantry away from the main assault in the centre, and additional subterfuge was provided from 6 February to the time of the crossings by the air forces of 221 Group, which put into effect Operation Cloak. Taking as its inspiration similar operations in the lead-up to the Normandy landings, dummy parachutists and devices known as 'canned battle' were dropped at various locations to confuse the defence. These devices, when hitting the ground, precisely imitated the sound of rifle fire interspersed with the detonation of grenades. Also deployed was the similar 'Aquakit' which, upon hitting water, sent up Very lights.

With the coming of dark on the night of 12 February assault troops, transport, organisation, signals and regulating headquarters moved into position without incident. Various modes of transport were available for the crossing, including local Burmese river craft. All would require rowing or towing, and in respect of the latter the miscellaneous collection of 'motorised' craft available amounted to:

- 120 assault boats with 9.8hp outboard motors
- 11 class 9 rafts with outboard motors
- 7 class 40 rafts with motor-boats and propulsion sets.[27]

With the equipment available, crossings of from 1,500 to in excess of 2,000 yards in prospect, a stiff breeze blowing and a current of 2–3 knots running, the unpleasant realisation dawned that oar power would be the principal form of propulsion.

A final check of the far bank was made after dark by detachments of the Special Boat Service and the Sea Reconnaissance Unit, during which two Japanese were discovered swimming in the river and had to be shot to prevent their escape. It is possible that this noise may have alerted the defence, however, the lead company of 2 Battalion, The South Lancashire Regiment, manned their boats and at 0343 hours left the west bank to row across the river, it still being considered essential that the first attempt be made in silence. Reaching the east bank undiscovered at 0515 hours the company made their way to the top of the bluffs and set up a defensive position.

Detachments of the Special Boat Service were now marking sandbanks in the river and beaches on the east bank with lights, but as the remainder of 2 Battalion prepared for their crossing problems began to arise. Due to the need for silence it had not been possible to warm up outboard motors in advance and many refused to start, in addition to which a number of boats were damaged during transportation in lorries over indifferent roads and discovered at the water's edge to be unserviceable. At 0430 hours the battalion started to cross but of the 'motorised' craft that it had been possible to start, many broke down in mid stream. The battalion contributed to their own misfortunes when the reserve company, which should have been last, found itself leading the crossing and instead of carrying on attempted to circle around to its proper position. Unfortunately the feeble motors in their boats were not strong enough for the current and they began to drift downriver. An estimated landing time of 0530 hours slipped by and the assault craft did not approach the opposite shore until 0610, well after daylight.

With the coming of daylight the battalion was subjected to a hail of fire from medium machine guns. Heavy casualties were taken and a number of boats were sunk while others began to drift down river past Japanese positions which kept them under heavy fire. IV Corps tanks and artillery on the west bank attempted to cover the assault but due to the need for secrecy their guns were not registered and their fire was necessarily slow and inaccurate until they found the range. Fighter support from a 'cab rank' circling above was called in and under covering fire some 2 Battalion boats grounded on a sand bank from which their occupants were later recovered, while other survivors, some swimming, returned to the west bank. The first attempt had failed, with the exception of the lead company, which now found itself isolated and in grave danger.

A further assault was required with the minimum possible delay and since too much time would be lost reorganising the South Lancs, 4 Battalion 15 Punjab were ordered to make the attempt a little farther upstream. Time was lost while damaged boats were repaired, however as secrecy was no longer a requirement outboard motors were properly warmed and tested, and under covering fire from the air plus tanks and artillery, the lead company left the west bank at 0945 hours and made the crossing without incident. By 1140 hours the whole of 4/15 Punjab were over the river, the company of 2 South Lancs already across began operations and by shortly after noon the few Japanese in evidence were cleared from the beach areas.

By nightfall of the 13th most of 33 Brigade were across, and by nightfall of the following day they were joined by the South Lancashires and 89 Brigade less 1/11 Sikh who were engaged elsewhere, as will be related. Some opposition was encountered, notably at the eastern end of Nyaungu village where heavy fighting took place. Defending infantry were also discovered in positions located in ancient catacombs to the south east of the village, from which they stubbornly refused to surrender. Having no time for niceties 7 Division troops sealed the entrances, and in the words of the official report the Japanese were 'left to contemplate the folly of their ways'.[28]

With troops and equipment pouring across the river at Nyaungu a properly prepared and defended bridgehead now rapidly became a reality.

To the south of Nyaungu at Pagan, 11/14 February was also an eventful time for 1 Battalion 11 Sikh Regiment, 89 Brigade. Ordered to make a crossing at that point, and yet without the boats to accomplish their mission as all those available to 7 Division were allocated to Nyaungu, the Sikhs were obliged to try to persuade local boatmen to take them across. The locals were not unnaturally less than keen on the enterprise but on 11 February were persuaded to ferry the patrol previously referred to across to the eastern bank. The patrol reported back that Pagan was unoccupied and it was decided that 1/11 Sikh should make their crossing in two movements, the first on the night of the 12/13th from the west bank to an island in the middle of the river, and the second, at daylight on the 14th from the island to the eastern bank.

During a pitch-black night the Sikhs were moved lock, stock, and barrel 300 yards to the island, ferried by six country boats, and by daylight the battalion was safely hidden in its concentration area. However, at around 1100 hours the patrol on the eastern bank reported that Pagan had now been occupied. Having been upgraded from a diversion to a full-blown crossing, the original intention of the operation – to draw the Japanese away from Nyaungu –

had been a resounding and, for the Sikhs, now a rather uncomfortable success. Since going back would undoubtedly attract as much attention as going forward, it was decided that the original plan would be adhered to and at 0400 14 February B Company set off for the eastern bank, once more in country boats ferried by local boatmen.

As they neared the eastern bank the boats were swept by a hail of machine gun fire, the boatmen immediately took refuge in the bottom of the boats and could not be persuaded to resume rowing. Unused to the unwieldy river craft the Sikhs were unable to control them and they drifted helplessly downstream until the boatmen could be persuaded to resume rowing and return to the island. B Company were fortunate to have had only one man wounded but it was evident that a further attempt in daylight would be impossible.

As they contemplated the eastern shore wondering how best to proceed, officers of 89 Brigade were surprised to see a small boat pull out from the opposite bank rowed by two INA soldiers bearing a white flag. Brought ashore, the two advised their bemused captors that the Japanese had left Pagan, marched upstream and left the defence to the Nehru Brigade, who for the most part showed little heart for the fight. 1/11 Sikh now pushed on across the river to Pagan meeting light opposition from the INA, some 280 of whom subsequently surrendered, while the remainder withdrew south.

The Japanese withdrawal seems on the face of it to be uncharacteristic, however at that time XXXIII Corps were stepping up the pressure and even at that late date, bereft as he was of air reconnaissance, such was the reduced state of the JAAF, Kimura remained convinced that he faced all of 14th Army at Mandalay where he believed the decisive battle of the war in Burma would be fought. He was in fact not unduly concerned at the crossings around Mandalay since he believed General Slim to be playing into his hands, the Japanese intention being to catch his opponent with his command split by the Irrawaddy, half on the west bank, half on the east bank and defeat each half in turn. Dismissing the crossings at Nyaungu and Pagan as demonstrations by not much more than the East Africans, who could be dealt with at a later date, he continued to draw his troops northward.

III

With the Mandalay front as their prime objective Kimura's forces hurled attack after attack at both the 19 and 20 Indian Division bridgeheads north of the city and to the south and west. Despite the enormous pressure on them both positions held and were expanded and consolidated.

Lieutenant General Slim originally intended fighting the Japanese on the plain of Shwebo but Kimura saw the dangers, refused to be drawn, and withdrew beyond the Irrawaddy. Slim had an alternative plan already in place, that now being put into operation, but it stretched his available forces to the limit, as a consequence of which he requested reinforcement in the shape of 36 British Division, presently with General Sultan's NCAC. The request was considered sympathetically but both Mountbatten and Leese feared that such a move would interfere with NCAC operations, in addition to which it would take some time for the division to be moved the long distance south.

Slim's only other source of reinforcement was 5 Indian Division, already under his command and at Jorhat since January being reorganised on an airborne and mechanised transport establishment similar to that of 17 Indian Division. The intention had always been to use the division during the campaign, probably as replacement for one of those already engaged, however it now became apparent that 5 Indian Division could well be needed in addition to those already engaged.

The 14th Army commander now faced a dilemma, and yet again it came down to supply. The air transport squadrons of CCTF upon whom XXXIII and IV Corps largely relied had been flying greatly extended hours and making a phenomenal effort for weeks to keep the advance going. Aircrew, ground crew, and the aircraft themselves had limits, and the question arose as to whether they would have the capacity to transport and supply an extra division? Slim could either leave 5 Division where they were and risk losing the battle for lack of available forces, or bring the division forward and risk having the battle collapse because he was unable to keep his available forces adequately supplied. He decided to bring the division forward and risk the logistical and administrative problems which inevitably arose:

Throughout the battle we were never without acute anxiety on the supply and transport side. Almost daily there was a crisis of some kind. The reserves of some basic ration would fall frighteningly low, guns would be silent for want of ammunition, river craft out of action for want of spares, wounded collecting in some hard-pressed spot with no means of evacuating them. Petrol was always desperately short. Yet we got over all these difficulties and a thousand others by juggling between formations with the limited transport available and by cruelly overworking the men who drove, flew, sailed, and maintained our transport of all kinds.[29]

The air transport system had many advantages, in particular the supply of fresh vegetables, mail (very important from a morale point of view) and canteen stores, but it also lacked something in terms of flexibility. Such was the rate of turn around for the aircraft that stores and equipment were stacked, loaded, and delivered in double quick time with little opportunity to take into consideration last minute changes. Staff officers, especially at brigade and division level, therefore needed to be well organised and able to forecast general demands some time in advance of actual requirement in order to ameliorate as far as possible the worst effects of the shortages that Slim refers to. Still, emergencies did of course occur. In one instance as 255 Indian Tank Brigade prepared to cross the Irrawaddy a defect was discovered affecting bogey wheels and idlers for their tanks. All transport aircraft were working at full capacity therefore there was some delay obtaining the requisite quantities of these these crucial but heavy items, and when they did arrive it was only at the expense of other stores and equipment already requested.[30]

17 Indian Division and 255 Indian Tank Brigade were ferried across the Irrawaddy into the 7 Division bridgehead 18/21 February, the 17 Division plan of operations for their crucial and necessarily rapid advance on Meiktila being divided into six phases:

1. Crossing of the Irrawaddy, capture of Ngathayauk, and exploitation to Welaung and Seiktein.
2. Capture of Mahlaing, sealing off or capture of Taungtha, concentration of the division in Mahlaing.

3. Capture of an airstrip at or near Meiktila for the fly-in of 99 Indian Infantry Brigade.
4. Isolation of Meiktila.
5. Capture of Meiktila.
6. Capture of Thazi.[31]

On 21 February 48 Indian Infantry Brigade struck out for Ngathayauk, a group of seven villages 16 miles (26km) from Nyaungu. With the tanks of 5 Horse and 9 Horse (255 Tank Brigade) operating to their south through Wetlu, these advance units were followed by the rest of the division. The road to Meiktila led through 82 miles (132km) of enemy held country and since a land based line of communications could not be maintained, the division sealed itself off as it proceeded, armoured cars in front, followed by tanks and the bulk of the infantry, the 3,000 vehicles of the column, and a rear guard of tanks and infantry. The division was to be supplied from the air.

Advancing through Ngathayauk, the division met light opposition and pressed on towards Taungtha, sappers in the advance busily engaged in making the chaungs in the area fit for crossing by vehicles. By 1130 hours 23 February the division had made good progress, reaching Seiktin without much interference from the Japanese, the principal problem in this arid plain of central Burma being water.

IV

23 February 1945 – a day, to use Lieutenant General Slim's own description, of 'horrors' for 14th Army's prospects. Battle had been joined from the NCAC front in north east Burma, through the furious battles now being fought around Mandalay and was about to erupt at Meiktila, the whole a concave front over 200 miles (322km) in length; and on this day Generalissimo Chiang Kai-shek, without prior warning, ordered the immediate return to China of all US and Chinese forces in NCAC, together with their attendant transport aircraft. NCAC was at this time a substantial force comprising three Chinese Divisions plus the Mars Brigade, a US/Chinese formation approximately the equivalent of a small division. Pending their withdrawal the Generalissimo stipulated that these forces should under no circumstances operate farther south than the

line Lashio/Hsipaw/Kyaukme, which would bring their advance to a halt some 80 miles (129km) north-east of Mandalay.

Lieutenant General Honda's assessment that China and the US had no real interest in Burma had proven uncannily accurate and the consequences for 14th Army were potentially catastrophic. Without the Chinese/US troops the only Allied unit remaining in the north eastern area would be 36 British Division, and Kimura would be free to turn all his available forces, estimated at some 50,000 men, against XXXIII Corps at Mandalay. To greatly compound his problems Slim was also notified that the USAAF transport squadrons supplying NCAC would be used to fly them out, while the 14th Army aircraft allocation would have to take on the additional task of supplying them while they awaited transportation to China. The loss of the NCAC troops was a major setback, but Slim considered the loss of the transport aircraft to be far more serious and a potentially fatal blow to the campaign. Both Slim and General Leese made impassioned protests to Admiral Mountbatten.

The Supreme Commander SEAC also received the bad tidings on 23 February in a telegraph message from Lieutenant General Sultan which informed him of the expected imminent receipt of orders to withdraw to China, and such was the nature of the crisis that on 8 March Mountbatten flew to Chungking to meet with Chiang Kai-shek personally. At their meeting Mountbatten outlined the essential nature of the campaign in progress, the importance to China of driving the Japanese from Burma, and not least the fact that without Chinese troops for its defence the security of the Ledo supply route from Assam to China would be gravely imperilled.

The Generalissimo remained unmoved. He planned a counter-offensive in China to recapture the provinces of Hunan and Kwangsi, the 'rice bowl' of that immense country, which provided most of the staple diet for a nation which now faced starvation. For the coming campaign, intended to start in the autumn, he proposed to form fifteen new divisions immediately, rising to thirty-nine US-equipped divisions, the essential nucleus of this vast array being the trained and experienced NCAC forces, particularly the Mars Brigade. To counter Mountbatten's continued protests Chiang Kai-shek proposed halting the advance at Mandalay until the outcome of the Chinese offensive was known, a course of action impossible to contemplate since it would entail 14th Army being supplied largely by air through the coming monsoon, due to start in May. Further argument with the Generalissimo proved useless and final orders for the immediate commencement of the withdrawal were issued 11 March.

The entire campaign in Burma now descended into a considerable state of uncertainty for 14th Army had to be in Rangoon by the start of monsoon to enable that port to be opened and supplies brought through in quantity. If that should now be considered impossible the Army would have to withdraw from Mandalay–Meiktila to secure its lines of communication, allowing Kimura months in which to replenish and reinforce his armies.

Even without the NCAC formations to assist him Lieutenant General Slim was confident that he could bring the campaign to a successful conclusion, but he could not under any circumstances contemplate the reductions in his transport aircraft allocation now being proposed. As has been related, the transport squadrons supporting 14th Army were already operating well beyond normal safety limits and had been for some time. XV Corps had been taken off air-supply completely to help make up the deficit and operations in the Arakan had suffered as a consequence, allowing Kimura to transfer troops from there to the Irrawaddy front.

Mountbatten made strong representations to the British Chiefs of Staff who in turn took the matter up with the US Joint Chiefs. To underline this approach Prime Minister Winston Churchill sent a personal message to the United States top soldier, General of the Army George C. Marshall, pointing out that the vigour with which the British/Indian forces in Burma had conducted operations had allowed the US to achieve its strategic goal of opening a land supply route from India to China. He also pointed out that three British/Indian divisions earmarked for Burma had been retained in Italy and that, as a consequence, it had been possible to send three British/Canadian divisions from Italy to reinforce General Eisenhower, to the great advantage of the campaign in Northern Europe. Prime Minister Churchill concluded by saying that, 'the comparatively small additional support' required for 14th Army, in the shape of the USAAF transport squadrons, would enable Rangoon to be reached before monsoon and the campaign in Burma virtually won.

General Marshall replied on 4 April that the US would not remove any of its transport squadron allocation for 14th Army before Rangoon was captured or 1 June, whichever was the sooner. This was something of a relief but the decision made by the US Administration still imposed a very strict timetable. Rangoon must be reached, captured, and in some sort of operation in less than two months or the US squadrons would be withdrawn and 14th Army might still be forced into a long and costly retreat.[32]

Despite all the turmoil Lieutenant General Slim still had a campaign to win, and the sooner the better.

Chapter 4

Meiktila: The Capture

I

Characteristically Slim decided to drive the campaign forward, not give the Japanese any respite, and let June 1 take care of itself.

Having reached Seiktin 23 February 17 Indian Division forged on to the capture of Taungtha and moved on toward Mingan with, for a brief period on the afternoon of the 24th, the entire division advancing rapidly on a broad front over bunds, cactus hedges and broken ground. Principal opposition encountered thus far had been snipers, over 100 of whom needed to be winkled out and dealt with before harbouring for the night could be completed. The 48 Indian Infantry Brigade remained at Taungtha 25 February to collect a supply drop, which was successfully delivered, while the remainder of the division moved on to the village of Mahlang, captured without opposition 0830 hours 26th.

The next major objective was Thabutkon. Situated 13 miles (21km) from Meiktila the airfield was earmarked for the receipt of rapid reinforcement in the shape of 99 Indian Infantry Brigade, the third 17 Division brigade and now established on a fully air transportable basis. At 0930 of the 26th tanks of 9 Horse, accompanied by armoured cars and 4 Battalion 4 Bombay Grenadiers, departed on a wide left hook over difficult ground peppered with the inevitable snipers, and captured the airfield during the early afternoon of the same day. The fly-in of the 4,000 men of 99 Brigade began in earnest on the 27th and over the next four and a half days, with Thabutkon still under fire, transport aircraft made an astonishing 655 trips to the airfield, the majority by squadrons of the USAAF, with six RAF squadrons giving invaluable support.

The principal objective of the entire campaign, the capture of Meiktila, now lay before the division.

Positioned on the Myingyan branch of the main railway line from Rangoon to Mandalay and points north, Meiktila was situated 320 miles (515km) from Rangoon and 75 miles (121km) from Myingyan. The principal feature of the town comprised a large artificial lake which was, for all practical purposes, divided into two expanses of water, the north and south lakes. Across the small strip of water uniting the two lakes lay a bridge to take the railway plus a narrow wooden bridge connecting the main built up area to the east of the lakes with the railway station to the west. To the south of the railway, and running parallel to it, a canal formed a formidable obstacle to the movement of tanks.

Scattered around Meiktila were five airfields, including Thabutkon, designed to protect the Japanese line of communications as far as the Irrawaddy. JAAF aircraft were now noticeably scarce. All that remained operational of *5th Hikoshidan* (Air Division), tasked with supporting Burma Area Army, was the *64th Hikosentai* (Flying Regiment), which had available no more than twenty Type 3 Ki-43 'Oscar' Fighters, plus nine Ki-48 'Lily' light bombers of *8th Hikosentai* and four heavy bombers of *58th Hikosentai* (although the *8th* and *58th* were in fact already under orders to proceed to the Siam/Indo China theatre). Quite apart from Meiktila itself, the airfields would be of immense value to 14th Army. Intelligence reports indicated that the main Japanese defences around Meiktila were approximately oval shaped some 3 miles (4.82km) wide at their maximum east to west and 4½ miles (7.24km) at their maximum north to south.

The question now arises as to what the Japanese were doing while all this activity was in progress, and it seems that in getting as far as they had, 17 Indian Division may have been the beneficiaries of an extraordinary piece of luck. Aware that enemy units were active in the Nyaungu/Pagan area, Kimura called another conference for his senior officers, this time at Meiktila itself, to assess the situation. Chaired by Major General Tanaka, Kimura's Chief of Staff, and attended by, among others, Lieutenant Generals Katamura of *15th Army*, and Honda of *33rd Army*, the conference soon degenerated into a row between Katamura and Honda on the one hand, who believed that a major operation was now under way to capture Meiktila, and Tanaka, who insisted that enemy forces in the area were light and posed no great threat. During the course of their heated debate Tanaka received a telegram stating that an enemy column of 200 vehicles was approaching, a small force that appeared to confirm the Burma Area Army Chief of Staff's assessment. Katamura and Honda had no option but to accept that they were wrong and the conference broke up. It subsequently transpired that the signal to Tanaka was garbled, '200 vehicles' should have read '2,000 vehicles' and referred to 17 Indian Division, which was advancing rapidly.[33]

With the capture of Thabutkon the penny at last dropped for at least one senior Japanese officer, the newly appointed commander of Meiktila and surrounding district, Major General Kasuya, although even he initially believed that the main attack would come from airborne troops. Kasuya commanded around 12,000 men although most were scattered over a wide area and included the snipers that were so troublesome to the Allied advance. Actually in Meiktila he had a disparate force comprising four airfield defence units, three infantry companies hastily scratched together from line of communication troops, various small administration units and between 400 and 500 'walking wounded' from the military hospital. Not a first rate command in the the usual sense but all could be expected to fight fanatically in the Japanese tradition, and die rather than surrender. At the last moment welcome reinforcement arrived for Kasuya in the shape of *1st Battalion, 168 Regiment, 49th Division*, plus an advance party from the rest of *168 Regiment* comprising approximately half the strength of each battalion but no guns. Also able to evade the tightening 17 Division grip and join the defence were *49 Mountain Artillery Regiment* and elements of *1 Independent Anti-Tank Battalion*. Documents captured after the battle showed Meiktila to have been defended by approximately 3,200 men, well armed and equipped.

Kasuya had another piece of good luck in having on hand a widely experienced infantryman, Major Araki, officer commanding *2 Battalion, 215 Regiment*, who happened to be in Meiktila with thirteen men of his unit. Araki was appointed to command the western sector of the defence, his orders to secure his outer line of defences, guard against any advance from the west either along the Kyaukpadaung road or the Myingyan railway axis, and keep in close touch with units of *5 Air Division*, which held advance positions to the north west. Command of the eastern sector was given to Major Nomaguchi with orders to secure his perimeter and destroy any forces attacking from the north down the Mahlaing road. Kasuya also organised a mobile strike force plus a reserve, and disposed his forces as follows:

Western sector
- No. 1 Emergency Infantry Company (L of C troops).
- No. 2 Emergency Infantry Company (L of C troops).
- Meiktila detachment Mobile Reserve Infantry.
- Detachment Meiktila section, Northwest branch, Burma Area Army Field Freight Depot.
- Various units of 33 Division left in Meiktila.
- 107 Line of Communication Hospital plus various small miscellaneous units.

1 Battalion 168 Regiment arrived by 27 February and was placed under the command of Major Araki, who positioned them in the south-west of the town astride the Kyaukpadaung road, which skirted the Mondaing Chaung. Battalion dispositions were 1 Company on the right, 3 Company on the left, 2 Company in the rear as reserve. The battalion gun platoon covered the 3 Company front. Battalion warning signals were red. Very light for tank attack, green for major attack developing.

When the advance party from the remainder of *168 Regiment* arrived some time around 28 February, they took up positions in the south of the town, probably in the eastern sector:

Eastern Sector
- 84 Airfield Battalion.
- 52 Airfield Battalion.
- 36 Anti Aircraft Battalion.
- 34 Special Duty Section (possibly commandos).
- All remaining air units in Meiktila.
- No. 3 Emergency Infantry Company (L of C troops).
- One platoon Mobile Reserve Infantry.
- Detachment Meiktila section, Northwest branch, Burma Area Army Field Freight Depot.
- Various small miscellaneous units.

Mobile Units
- KISO Tai (indeterminate strength) O/C Captain Kawakami.
- One section Mobile Reserve Infantry in light motor transport.

Reserve
- Three detachments Mobile Reserve Infantry.

The *49 Mountain Artillery Regiment* and *1 Independent Anti-Tank Battalion* components were placed in the heavily built up cantonments area in the south-eastern sector of the town, and around the railway line.[34]

Major General Kasuya proved to be an able and energetic commander, and having made his dispositions ordered an extensive network of minefields prepared, particularly in the eastern sector. He also put in place the mining of bridges and causeways, the preparation of booby traps, planting of aircraft bombs as mines, the building of new bunkers, improvement of old ones, and the deployment of his anti-aircraft battalion in an anti-tank role.

Mines placed by the Japanese along the approaches to Meiktila tended to be few in number and of little value. In Meiktila itself many of the mines were actually aerial bombs which no longer had the aircraft to drop them. These would usually be buried but in some instances would be left in view in the middle of a road to drive tanks into nests of mines along the verges. Methods of detonating these explosives fell into three categories:

1. Pressure of a vehicle on a board covering the bomb's nose fuse.
2. Electric detonator with remote control.
3. Detailing a man armed with a hammer or rock to sit in the same hole as the bomb.

There is also evidence that 'lunge' mines were used against tanks. These suicide weapons were first encountered by US troops on Leyte, and weighing in at 16.5lb (7.48kg) with an explosive charge of around 6lb 9oz (3kg) were so-called because the soldier carrying the mine would lunge in a manner rather like striking out with a bayonet on the end of a rifle, to drive the detonator in the nose of the mine head on against the target.

Booby traps were based around an explosive mix of picric acid placed either in sandbags or wooden boxes with a detonator (often a grenade) connected to, for example, a trip wire or a selection of risqué postcards. As a final gesture Kasuya opened the extensive ordnance depots east of the north lake to all-comers, issuing mainly automatic weapons and ammunition. He then ordered the depots destroyed, fires from the burning buildings being visible to 17 Division advance units on the ridges 7 miles north west of the town on 27 February.

Despite Kasuya's largesse with the weaponry under his control, some defenders still did not have guns. Patients at the 107 Line of Command Hospital, for instance, were turned out of bed and told that there were no rifles for them so they would be required to fashion spears from bamboo. One prisoner of war and several dead were subsequently found to be in possession of these crude weapons.

II

Intelligence reports to Major General D.T. Cowan, GOC 17 Indian Division, indicated that Meiktila was, unlike initial expectations, heavily defended, and that approaches to the town from the west, in which the lakes featured strongly, would be the most problematical. His difficulties were further compounded by the fact that large groups of Japanese roamed the countryside attempting to join the defence, therefore the task before 17 Division was to make a quick, clean, capture of the town and the airfield on its eastern outskirts. Should significant enemy reinforcement effect an entry into Meiktila, its capture could become a long drawn-out affair with a number of unpleasant consequences for 14th Army, not least the approach of monsoon in May followed by 1 June and withdrawal of the USAAF transport squadrons.

Cowan's solution was to send mobile detachments to ring the town and block main roads, despatch 255 Indian Tank Brigade on a flanking movement to deliver their attack from the east while 48 Indian Infantry Brigade attacked along the axis of the Mahlaing road from the north, and 63 Indian Infantry Brigade moved in from the west (see map on p.xv) A divisional artillery harbour was established at the village of Antua, from where the guns could cover any assault from any direction. RAF forward observation units equipped with ground-to-air radio and 'embedded' with the infantry moved forward to draw down air strikes when and where necessary.

The attack commenced 28 February when 63 Brigade, leaving one battalion to guard the artillery, moved forward on foot, leaving all non-essential transport at Thabutkon. Patrols were sent forward to probe Japanese defences and reports came back that the western edge of Meiktila was held in force. With the approach of darkness the brigade halted at Kyaukpyugon.

On the same day 48 Brigade reached the Mahlaing/Meiktila road where 1 Battalion 7 Gurkha Rifles proceeded on foot, leading the advance south. Held up by light and medium machine gun fire, the battalion was also required to negotiate a partly demolished bridge across a chaung. With darkness coming on, at 2150 hours the Gurkhas sent two companies across the chaung to gain a foothold in the town. These companies subsequently withdrew to the north of the chaung, but later that night one company returned to Meiktila to probe the defences and was held up at a defensive strong point in and around a monastery on the northern outskirts of the town.

With the farthest distance to travel, 255 Tank Brigade despatched two reconnaissance columns, each comprising a squadron of 9 Horse tanks, a troop of armoured cars, two platoons of infantry, and a detachment of Royal Engineers. Both columns encountered difficult ground and were delayed by bridges rigged for demolition, however column A reached its objective on the Meiktila/Mandalay road without incident. B column pressed on across the airfield to the east of the town, bumping into defending infantry hidden in dense scrub in the canal/level crossing area and becoming heavily engaged due south of Khanda and the railway line. Tanks found the canal impossible to cross and were ordered to withdraw to nearby high ground from which it was hoped that they might give covering fire to the main brigade attack.

This attack was to be made by the tanks of 5 Horse supported by 6 Battalion 7 Rajput, who, from a forming up point at Khanda, were to advance either side of the railway line. The attack went forward on a two squadron, two company front, the right forward squadron and company deploying successfully, their left equivalent coming under heavy machine gun fire from a nulla as they crossed the railway line to form up, the Rajput infantry suffering severe casualties as a result. The left squadron commander moved one troop of tanks onto the line of the nulla while a second troop moved onto a road running parallel to, and south of, the railway line. The commander of this second troop reported few enemy infantry but that petrol drums were being set afire all around and that his tanks were in danger. Opening his tank hatch to raise up for a better look, the troop commander was killed instantly by sniper fire.[35]

Meanwhile the troop of tanks along the nulla engaged and destroyed a number of Japanese bunkers, however, on trying again to advance, accompanying infantry once more suffered casualties and were forced to withdraw. The deadly symphony of battle engulfed the northern perimeter of the town, the bone-jarring bass of the artillery joined by the clanking score of tank tracks and the rattle and crack of machine gun and small arms fire.

With the coming of night Major General Cowan was reluctant to leave his tanks in amongst the smouldering ruins and withdrew them to harbour 2 miles outside the town, leaving strong points to hold gains made thus far. During the night Japanese infantry filtered back into areas they had lost during the day and a fierce fire fight continued at point-blank range until dawn.

Slim, meanwhile, had been at Mandalay overseeing the XXXIII Corps break-out timed to coincide with the IV Corps assault on Meiktila. With coordination of the two attacks an essential component of his plan, he became concerned that the attack at Meiktila had stalled and decided to take a look for himself. On the morning of 1 March the 14th Army commander attempted to get a flight down to the IV Corps front and became somewhat hot under the collar when the RAF politely but firmly informed him that they would not fly him down to Meiktila as it was far too dangerous! Whoever the RAF officer was that faced Lieutenant General Slim at the charge must have been a brave man – and the RAF did have a point. Reinforcements were being landed at Thabutkon but the airstrip was still under heavy attack from Japanese ground forces and JAAF fighters were also in evidence. With ground and air battles swirling all around the airstrip and the only other suitable candidate, the airfield to the east of Meiktila, not yet fully in 17 Division hands, flying the commanding general in would not be sound military practice by any stretch of the imagination. But Slim was not a man to take 'no' for an answer.

On the verge of giving Air Vice-Marshal Vincent, AOC 221 Group, his forthright opinion, Slim was presented with another opportunity. A visiting US General arrived at 14th Army HQ Mandalay with his own Mitchell bomber, and Slim asked him if he would like to see something of the Meiktila battle in company with the commanding general. Delighted to accept the offer, and with typical American generosity, the visitor suggested that they go in his aircraft, and Slim gratefully accepted!

Flying down to Pagan, the group picked up Lieutenant General Messervy and flew on to an airstrip close to Thabutkon which, mercifully, was relatively quiet at the time. Cowan sent a couple of jeeps to pick up the visitors and transport them to his headquarters where Slim, greatly impressed by the way his divisional commander handled the difficult battle, was reassured.[36]

III

On that same morning, 1 March, the battle for Meiktila reopened with renewed ferocity. In the 63 Brigade area 1 Battalion 10 Gurkha Rifles were ordered to attack the village of Kanna, west of Meiktila. Two companies of Gurkhas duly went forward supported by a troop of 5 Horse tanks, cleared the village and continued toward Meiktila with a tank to protect each flank. The left company ran into heavy sniping from the jail, and tanks were called in to clear the way. The right company, meanwhile, entered the hospital compound where the Japanese had constructed numerous bunkers, the occupants of which offered fanatical resistance. Air strikes were called in which blasted the bunkers and set the hospital afire, reportedly killing 50–60 Japanese inside.

Assaulted by aerial bombs and artillery shells, the dry Burma plain erupted into swirling clouds of dust through which the protagonists sought each other with deadly intent. As the battle entered the town, falling masonry, the 'crump' of exploding grenades and the 'zip' and 'spat' of ricochets added to a cacophony of sound to assail the ears.

To the north, 1 Battalion, 7 Gurkha Rifles, 48 Brigade, supported by two squadrons of 9 Horse tanks, advanced down the Mandalay road on a two company front. The advance went well until the battalion approached a monastery and bungalow in the northern suburbs. Here tenacious resistance was encountered, the area only being cleared following heavy fighting and the detonation of a 250lb bomb inside the monastery. Now entering a densely populated area, the Gurkhas encountered large numbers of Japanese machine gun positions placed in houses, the resultant crossfires being particularly troublesome and the positions requiring clearance house by house. Aerial bombs dug into the roads further delayed the advance, as did a number of 'dummy' minefields consisting of nothing more than bricks lightly covered with earth. Finally, at dusk, the Gurkhas reached a position approximately 100 yards (91m) north of the railway line, and at 1800 hours they were ordered to withdraw for the night to Kyigon.[37]

On the 255 Indian Tank Brigade front to the east, a force commanded by Lieutenant Colonel Tighe comprising 4 Battalion 4 Bombay Grenadiers (minus two companies), the tanks of 9 Horse (minus the two squadrons with 48 Brigade), and a detachment of Royal Engineers advanced astride the railway line, their objective to probe in strength as far as the eastern end of the causeway to establish in what strength the enemy held the town centre. Meeting little resistance initially this force pressed on to within 200 yards (363m) of the railway station when they were held up by stiffer opposition. On the point of putting into operation a plan to capture the station Lieutenant Colonel Tighe was ordered to withdraw as the 48 Brigade attack already described was in progress and it was felt that having two separate commands in the centre of town would hamper rather than assist matters, and there was always the risk that casualties might be caused by 'friendly' fire if the two commands were to fire over their enemy and into each other's perimeters.

A Squadron 9 Horse were ordered to capture high ground to the south west of Meiktila and were obliged to deal with numerous enemy bunkers on the way to their objective. 5 Horse sent a squadron forward supported by 6 Battalion 7 Rajput to take this same position, which they did despite continuous heavy sniping. A Squadron 9 Horse, meanwhile, received orders to make a sweep to the south of the lake toward the Kyaukpadaung road in order to complete envelopment of the town. Held up attempting to cross a chaung via two bridges, one damaged and the other mined, A Squadron were ordered back to the assistance of 6/7 Rajput, which had come under heavy attack.

At the chaung a detachment of 36 Field Squadron, supported by a company of 6/7 Rajput, set-to clearing the mined bridge having put the infantry company across to keep snipers at a respectable distance. With the bridge 'deloused' the A Squadron tanks would be able to resume their advance the following day.[38]

On the morning of 2 March, west of Meiktila, 63 Brigade sent forward a company of 1 Battallion 10 Gurkha Rifles, supported by a squadron of 5 Horse tanks and fighter-bombers from the 'cab-rank' permanently in attendance above, to clear the area of the jail as far as the causeway. Mortar fire directed onto the jail building brought no response and tanks breached the walls, but it was found to be empty. Continuing on to the causeway the tanks came under heavy fire from 75mm guns located at the eastern end, two tanks receiving direct hits. Unable to continue in that direction, the attack was switched to further clearance of built up areas of the south-western sector.

Following an artillery barrage, the 5 Horse tanks advanced through dense thorn thickets and substantial stone buildings, the whole area dotted with vehicle pits, fox-holes and air raid shelters. The accompanying Gurkhas found it impossible to keep pace due to heavy sniper fire, nevertheless the tanks continued, the left troop entering a belt of scrubland 150 yards (137m) deep and coming under heavy small arms fire. Japanese infantry detailed as tank hunters targeted two of the tanks, hurling petrol bombs and placing explosive charges on the tracks. One tank was disabled but the remainder continued to blast every bunker they came across, debouching from the scrub to find the Japanese withdrawing across open ground to their front. Heavy casualties were inflicted on the disappearing enemy.

The right troop, meanwhile, advanced across relatively open ground blasting Japanese bunkers and calling in air support as and where necessary. Japanese resistance finally centred on a large red house with a deep air raid shelter, this building being shattered by a crossfire from the advancing 5 Horse tanks and a troop on the Kyaukpadaung road.[39]

At 1015 hours 2 March 48 Brigade to the north of Meiktila sent forward 4 Battalion 12 Frontier Force supported by B and C Squadrons 9 Horse, the tanks formed in a line east to west in the monastery area as the assault began. Stiff opposition was soon encountered from snipers and light machine gun positions in bunkers, but the advance continued slowly and steadily until, reaching a point some 50 yards (46m) from the railway, the tanks were fired on by 75mm guns south of the railway line. Well sited and well hidden the Japanese guns knocked out three tanks before they were located.

Despite the anti-tank fire, tanks and infantry continued over the railway line and it is believed that at least one of the 75mm guns was destroyed in this engagement, although the others remained in action. The tanks now came to the canal and found it impossible to cross, the only bridges being heavily mined, therefore C squadron on the left despatched one troop, supported by a platoon of infantry, eastwards against determined opposition to cross the canal by the eastern loop road, thence to fight their way westwards once more until the Japanese had been driven into the south-western area of the town. With the coming of night 48 Brigade and the 9 Horse tanks were withdrawn to defended harbour areas, leaving strong points to hold gains made.

The idea of withdrawing from positions hard won may seem counter-productive, but it reflects on the battlefield Slim's overall strategy, which was always to destroy the enemy, the acquisition of territory being very much a secondary objective. The whole Mandalay/Meiktila campaign was designed to finish Kimura's Burma Area Army as a fighting unit once and for all, and as far as the defenders of Meiktila were concerned, they had two clear alternatives: (1) they could surrender and (2) if they did not they would be taken on and dealt with in whichever part of the town they were found.

IV

The night of 2/3 March followed the same pattern as every other night since the opening of the attack. Japanese 'jitter' parties emerged from bunkers and foxholes to harass 17 Division troops in and around Meiktila and destroy any vehicles left outside comparatively safe harboured positions.

The morning of 3 March found the defenders much reduced in number but those remaining still determined to fight to the end. The principal attack this day was made in three phases by 48 Brigade from the north, for which 1 Battalion West Yorks relieved 4 Battalion 12 Frontier Force. At 0830 hours the first phase commenced when a company of West Yorks advanced from the monastery accompanied by A Squadron 9 Horse, reaching the railway line relatively easily. With the defence now principally confined to the south-west of the town, the second phase opened with heavy artillery and aerial bombardment of the area, followed at 1030 hours with an attack by a further company of West Yorks, supported by B Squadron 9 Horse, delivering a 'left hook' by crossing the railway line and canal at the eastern end of the town and attacking from north-east to south-west against heavy opposition.

The third phase of the operation began when, at 1300 hours, the first company of infantry and A Squadron crossed the railway line and canal, sappers having made safe the mined bridges, to support the left hook. With fanatical courage Japanese resistance continued unabated and a third company of West Yorks was deployed. Each building and bunker contained snipers or machine gun nests or both, and required clearance one by one in street fighting as vicious and deadly as anything encountered in any theatre of the war. Japanese 75mm guns engaged tanks at point blank range, knocking out three, two of which were completely destroyed. Overshooting became a major hazard as 63 Brigade held the area immediately west of the lake, and there were one or two dangerous incidents although no casualties were reported.

Building by building, street by street, the West Yorks and their tank support inched forward, in the process destroying six enemy 75mm guns and a 37mm anti-tank weapon. By 1700 hours the town area had been cleared, and at 1750 remaining defenders penned into gun emplacements on a promontory were finally overcome, some fifty jumping into the lake where they drowned or were killed rather than surrender.[40]

The four days fighting had been bitter, hand-to-hand, and to the death, and Meiktila was a shambles. In one small area some 200 yards by 100 yards, 876 Japanese bodies were counted. Of Major General Kasuya there was no sign, and in all likelihood he lay buried in one of the destroyed bunkers in the town. Very few of his command survived.

The battle had been a complicated one for it did not only entail capturing the town. Severely hampering the operation were the large numbers of Japanese roaming around outside who put up fierce resistance whenever and wherever they were encountered.

Many a bitter no-quarter engagement erupted in the surrounding villages and countryside.

Being much less dependent on motorised transport than 14th Army the Japanese used horses and mules in large numbers, in addition to which they corralled live cattle in the vicinity to supply fresh meat. Terrified, these animals ran amok to be slaughtered wholesale by artillery fire and air attack, their swollen carcasses lying where they died, host to dark billowing clouds of flies, infested with maggots and devoured by vultures. Meiktila resembled a charnel house. The stench was appalling.

V

Two VCs were won at Meiktila, both posthumous, one to Lieutenant W.B. Weston of The Green Howards, attached to 1 West Yorks, on 3 March, and one to Naik Fazal Din of 7 Battalion 10 Baluch, a day earlier.

At last Meiktila belonged to 17 Indian Division, and now they had to hold it.

Chapter 5

The Road From Mandalay

I

The fall of Meiktila took General Kimura completely by surprise. Aware that the town was under attack he held to the belief that it was only a diversionary assault to take his attention away from Mandalay; but with the realisation that a powerful enemy force now lay across his lines of communication and that his principal administration and supply base was in their hands, he reacted quickly and a spate of orders from HQ Burma Area Army altered the focus of Operation Ban from Mandalay and the Irrawaddy to Meiktila: *18th Division* was reassigned from the reinforcement of *15th Army* to the immediate recapture of Meiktila, *49th Division* was to march with all speed from Toungoo to cooperate in the attack under the overall command of Lieutenant General Naka, Officer Commanding *18th Division*. Also withdrawn from *15th Army* and sent south were *119th Infantry Regiment* (two battalions), *Naganuma Artillery Group* (nine 105mm guns and two 149mm howitzers), an anti-tank battalion, *Sakuma Force* (two battalions of the *214th Infantry Regiment*), *14th Tank Regiment* (approximately nine tanks), and various artillery units.[41]

Kimura was no longer under any illusion. If Meiktila could not be recaptured he would be unable to hold on at Mandalay and risked the destruction of *Burma Area Army* and the loss of Burma in its entirety.

The Japanese military were not tank minded in the same way as their European counterparts, believing that, in the territories and terrain in which they were likely to be fighting, tanks would be subordinate to the more traditional arms, rather than being weapons of decision in their own right. Nevertheless, Kimura was every bit as aware as Slim that the relatively flat central plain of Burma between Mandalay and Meiktila was 'good tank country', and he placed the only tank regiment at his disposal, the *14th* referred to above, around Myinmu, where, until Meiktila fell, he expected the main 14th Army attack to come.

14th Regiment would have mustered significantly more than nine tanks as it trundled south, but for the RAF. The Second World War saw the burgeoning of ground support from the air as a major component in the winning of campaigns, led by the ground breaking example of close cooperation that existed between the Luftwaffe and Wehrmacht in the early years of the war.

Patrolling above the Mandalay battle area, two Hurricanes, one piloted by Flight Lieutenant James Farquharson, the other by Flight Lieutenant R.J. Ballard, kept close contact with RAF Visual Control Posts accompanying their infantry below, but receiving no news of specific targets, instead received an intriguing warning to be on the lookout for Japanese armour. Of the two airmen, Farquharson in particular had an enviable reputation as a reconnaissance pilot and soon spotted what he believed might well be tank tracks disappearing into thick scrub. Radioing his find to Ballard and the VCPs, Farquharson was joined by the second Hurricane and the two circled the area until they spotted what appeared to be a small native hut in a nullah, the hut camouflaged by tree branches – although there were no trees around.

Farquharson fired a couple of cannon shells which blew away the branches to reveal a tank. The Hurricane proved itself to be a superb ground support aircraft in Burma, its 40mm cannon ideal for disposing of anything from vehicles to locomotives, although opportunities for 'tank busting' were rare. The two pilots therefore determined to make the most of this one, destroyed the tank and continued their search, calling up reinforcements in the process. During the course of that day thirteen of *14th Regiment*'s tanks were discovered and destroyed by cannon or rocket fire in what proved to be the heaviest concentration of Japanese armour in the entire campaign for Burma. That being the case, relying solely on camouflage for protection must be considered a serious error, for no anti-aircraft guns were in evidence until the following day – when it was too late.

II

With the battle for Meiktila reaching a crescendo in the early days of March, Slim needed to keep up the pressure on Mandalay, making

Kimura's withdrawal of troops from that sector to reinforce Meiktila a high risk strategy. As has been said, Slim's objective was above all the destruction of Japanese forces, and the 14th Army commander had plans in place for what he described as a 'hammer and anvil' operation, XXXIII Corps the hammer striking down from Mandalay toward the anvil, IV Corps at Meiktila, and the bulk of *Burma Area Army* caught between.

With this objective in view, 26 February saw 19 Indian Division (Officer Commanding Major General T.W. Rees) break out of the Kyaukmyaung bridgehead to the north of Mandalay, 64 and 62 Brigades smashing through the encircling *15 Division* and heading rapidly toward open tank country while the division's third unit, 98 Brigade, broke out of its bridgehead farther north at Thabeikyin and hurried to catch up, scattering the remnants of *15 Division* as it advanced.

Encountering pockets of stiff but uncoordinated resistance, the three brigades pushed rapidly south and by 6 March 62 Brigade, closely followed by 64 Brigade which had made a sweep to the east, was at Yenatha 8 miles (5km) north-east of Madaya, while 98 Brigade was crossing the Chuangmagyi, the last natural obstacle before Mandalay, between 62 Brigade and the Irrawaddy.

Madaya was a good sized town of about 10,000 inhabitants and the railhead for the Mandalay railway. It was also connected to its larger neighbour to the south by a good fair weather road, and while the railway terminated at the town the road carried on to the north, the direction from which 19 Indian Division approached. Madaya was strongly defended, with bunkered positions all around the perimeter but particularly to the north, from where the main assault was expected. Major General Rees, however, had other ideas and despatched an armoured column from 98 Brigade along the bank of the Irrawaddy to attack the town from the west.

Leading the column was 2 Battalion, Royal Berkshire Regiment, with 'B' Company in the van. The company made its way carefully along the approach to the town, a barely discernible track surrounded by swampy ground liberally covered with kunai grass 10 feet high that effectively reduced visibility to nil. Company Major John Hill sent a small reconnaissance party forward, and the company runner to the rear to make contact with Battalion HQ. Plunging into the long grass, the runner was never seen again. No shots were heard and it was assumed that he either became trapped in the swamp or was surprised by an enemy patrol.

On 7 March 'B' Company made its way over the remaining 2 miles (3.2km) to the town and entered the western outskirts. Signs of occupation were much in evidence but of the defenders themselves there was none. Major General Rees plan had worked, the main Japanese positions to the north were outflanked and the defence taken completely by surprise. Organising themselves into a defensive perimeter astride the main road to Mandalay, 'B' Company at last caught sight of the enemy approaching in groups of 200 to 300, and apparently completely oblivious to the fact that the town was no longer held by friendly forces.

Major Hill ordered the company to open fire and the Japanese scattered in all directions, screaming in surprise and leaving dead and wounded in their wake. A number of attempts were made to launch a concerted attack on the Royal Berkshire position, but these were broken up by company mortar fire. Several small parties of Japanese, however, were able to manoeuvre themselves close to the defensive perimeter and hurl in grenades. One of these parties, three men with a light machine gun, managed to infiltrate a house overlooking a chaung across which a bridge led from the perimeter to Battalion HQ. The first that 'B' Company knew of their presence was when one of the Japanese ran from the house to be shot down by Major Hill and several others simultaneously.

In an upstairs room the remaining two enemy soldiers, who must have known that they had no way out, remained where they were and fired at anything they saw but caused only one casualty, the wounding of one of the HQ Company complement, who was quite out of sight but hit by a ricochet. In an attempt to dislodge them, platoon Sergeant Scrivener attempted to lob two smoke grenades into the window of the occupied room but these unpredictable weapons bounced back and caused a fire which subsequently destroyed a large part of the town. With the house itself unaffected, Sergeant Scrivener gained entry covered by two members of his platoon, made his way stealthily upstairs and threw two grenades into the room, killing both Japanese.[42]

A feature of the action in Madaya was the number of stray chickens running loose with much squawking and flapping of wings. It was noticeable that as time progressed the noise from the chickens grew less and less, although Major Hill did not feel obliged to investigate their fate too closely!

With 'B' Company reinforced by the remainder of the column the town was successfully secured and the advance continued, 98 Brigade along the railway line with 64 Brigade about a mile to the east, until the outskirts of Mandalay were reached.

Japanese units were scattered throughout the city, 98 Brigade encountering particularly heavy resistance on Mandalay Hill, rising to some 800 feet (244m) in the north eastern sector, its steep slopes covered with substantial concrete temples and pagodas, heavily defended, honeycombed with machine gun positions and deep bunkers, and well supplied. During the night of 8/9 March 4/4 Gurkha scaled the north-eastern end of the hill and with the coming of dawn charged with kukris[43] drawn to engage in no-quarter hand-to-hand combat with defenders who fought with the desperation of men with nowhere to retreat, and who yet would not surrender. The following day the Gurkhas were reinforced by C and D Companies, 2 Battalion, The Royal Berkshire Regiment and the summit finally reached, but only after many of the defenders, holding out in deep tunnels and passageways, had to be burnt out by rolling down barrels of tar and oil and setting them afire with grenades and tracer bullets. By 11 March Mandalay Hill was in 98 Brigade hands but the difficult and dangerous job of mopping up, entailing winkling defenders out of concrete bunkers and tunnels, took a further eleven days.

Detailed to 'clear the west of Mandalay City' as its sister companies fought their way up the Hill, B Company, 2 Battalion, Royal Berkshire Regiment was again in action and advanced into the battle scarred expanse of the northern perimeter on what Major Hill believed might make a reasonable mission for a brigade, much less a rifle company reduced by hard campaigning to less than eighty men. Support came from A Company on its left plus mortar and artillery fire.

B Company immediately ran into nests of Japanese entrenched in bunkers and houses, but by nightfall of the 10th had advanced 600 yards (548m) and rested opposite the northern edge of Mandalay Hill. At dawn the following day the company began their cautious advance once more, one platoon or section giving covering fire while its companions moved forward. No. 5 Platoon engaged a

Japanese post to their front only to come under fire from a house already bypassed. Ordered up in support, a troop of tanks soon found itself moved elsewhere, and in built up areas the like of which which B Company now traversed, the effectiveness of their mortar and artillery support was significantly reduced.

Warily edging further into the city, the Company drew level with the massive walls of Fort Dufferin, in view about 600 yards to their left, and shortly thereafter were engaged by, and overcame, two light machine gun posts sited in a derelict building. Arriving at a high clock tower almost opposite the west gate of the fort, a halt was called – 2½ miles (4km) from their dawn starting point. The deadly game of hide and seek continued for the rest of the day, the grim butcher's bill amounting to eighteen Japanese dead, plus four of B Company killed, eleven wounded.[44] In five months of campaigning this one Company were in close quarter combat with the Japanese for eighty-six consecutive days. Of the original complement of 196 officers and men, 112 were killed or wounded. Their experience was replicated across 14th Army.

Surrounded by a wide moat, Fort Dufferin was a sizeable rectangular enclosure containing 1¼ square miles of parkland, barracks, official residences and the magnificent teak built Royal Palace of Thebaw, the last of the Burmese kings. Surrounding walls, of brick construction, were 30 feet (9m) wide at the base tapering to 12 feet (3.65m) at the top, forming a ramp protected by brick battlements 2–3 feet thick. The wall stood 23 feet (7m) high and was buttressed every 100 yards. Each wall had a main gate in the centre, set at an oblique angle to the bridge approaching across the moat and protected from direct fire by a massive buttress. In March 1945 this formidable fortification became the position of last resort for the Japanese in Mandalay. The problem for 14th Army was that they were comparatively lightly equipped and in any event did not have time to burn reducing fortifications with artillery fire. Consequently the fort was subjected to attacks reminiscent of the Napoleonic wars, with 'forlorn hope' storming parties in rafts paddling across the moat armed with scaling ladders.

First to try to gain entry were 8 Frontier Force Regiment, 98 Brigade, who attacked across the bridge to the northern gate with two troops of tanks. Heavy sniper and anti-tank fire was encountered, and one tank knocked out by a direct hit. The attack was

tenant General (later Field Marshal Viscount) Sir William Slim, G.C.B., G.C.M.G., G.C.V.O.,
E., D.S.O., M.C. at Monywa, 1945. (*IWM SE 3310*)

A Gurkha soldier crosses the Irrawaddy during the drive on Meiktila. He keeps his equipment d
by carrying it on his shoulders slung by a band over his head. *(IWM IND 4516)*

An Indian sapper engaged in the difficult and dangerous search for mines and booby traps durir
the approach to Meiktila. *(IWM IND 4479)*

...dian Infantry Brigade armoured column in the Nyaungu area. (*IWM IND 3071*)

...rt tanks about to cross into the XXXIII Corps bridgehead near Myinmu 12/13 February.
...waddy 2,000 yards wide at this point. (*IWM IND 4461*)

A Lee tank of 2 British Division comes ashore having been ferried across the Irrawaddy. (*IWM SE 3*

A West African Ascari tries the telephone in a captured Japanese foxhole. (*IWM IND 4239*)

waddy crossing point for 1 Battalion, 11 Sikh Regiment, 89 Indian Brigade, showing historic Pagan he opposite bank and the island used as a jumping off point on 13 February 1945. *(IWM IND 4470)*

ish self-propelled bridge. With a 'scissor' bridge already in place over a chaung near Meiktila, a :ially adapted Churchill tank carries a similar bridge across. *(IWM IND 3422)*

Japanese 'tankette' or light tank (3 to 4.5 tons depending upon type). Not particularly fast but a power to weight ratio of 25 resulted in good cross-country speeds. (*IWM STT 8212*)

Japanese 105mm howitzer. (*IWM MH 579*)

anese Mk.IX 75mm high velocity field gun with a range of 16,500 yards. (*IWM SE 3695*)

anese armoured recovery tank. (*IWM SE 3696*)

A Sikh patrol engages a Japanese foxhole in the Pagan area. The smoke is from a phosphorous grenade thrown a minute earlier. (*IWM IND 4550*)

A Priest self-propelled gun in action near Meiktila. A 105mm gun mounted on a Sherman tank chassis, the Priest proved itself a valuable weapon in Burma. (*IWM SE 3278*)

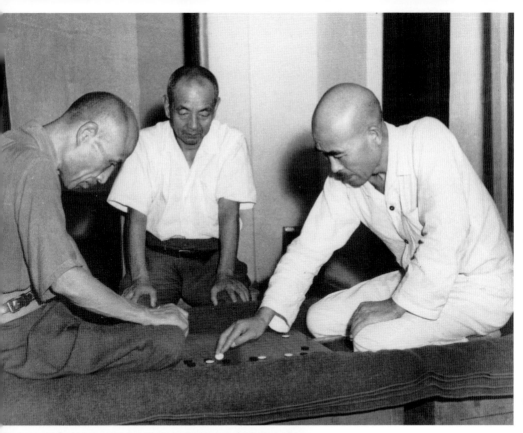

Lieutenant General Masaki Honda, Commander 33rd Army (right), with Lieutenant General Hayashi (left) and Major General Koba. (*IWM SE 6866*)

Field Marshal Count Juichi Terauchi, Japanese Supreme Commander South East Asia and Admiral Mountbatten's opposite number. (*IWM GER 83*)

3-inch mortars in action amid the pagodas of Meiktila. (*IWM SE 3283*)

Japanese attack on the cantonment area of Meiktila. Some of the 281 bodies counted the morning after the attack. (*IWM IND 4592*)

The wreckage of Meiktila railway station, focus for a number of hard fought actions. (*IWM SE 3291*)

British infantryman cautiously approaches Japanese foxhole on the outskirts of Meiktila. (*IWM SE 3108*)

Some of the few Allied landing craft left in theatre land XV Corps troops and equipment during t vital capture of Ramree Island. (*IWM IND 4432*)

Assault landing craft of the Indian Navy beaching in a narrow chaung in the Ru-Ywa area of the Arakan. (*IWM IND 4500*)

Battle scarred street in the Fort Dufferin area of Mandalay.
(*IWM IND 4536*)

The road from Mandalay. Ground crew 152 Squadron, RAF, leave Mandalay for Meiktila and Rangoon.
(*Ronald White*)

Yewe Village near Yindan, 12 miles S.E. of Meiktila. Troops move cautiously forward, tree to tree over bullet-swept ground, as a tank blasts a Japanese foxhole at point-blank range. (*IWM IND 4581*)

Monsoon. Digging drainage ditches in an attempt to keep torrential downpours from flooding the campsite. (*Ronald White*)

ive style 'basha' hut adopted by Allied servicemen in Burma. (*Ronald White*)

nsshipment of ammunition, Dakota transport to truck at a forward airstrip. (*IWM SE 3087*)

Reconnaissance photograph of Meiktila taken 30 January 1945. Clearly visible are the north and south artificial lakes. The railway enters the town from

called off and 8 Frontier Force dug in opposite the gate some 50 yards (45m) from the wall.

Inevitably, Slim's 'ace in the hole' – air power – was brought into play, and over several days the fortifications were extensively bombed to create a breach, until, on the morning of 20 March a group of Anglo-Burmese residents, waving white flags and Union Jacks, appeared at one of the gates to report that the Japanese garrison had escaped during the night through drains leading from the moat to the south of the town. Most were hunted down and rounded up, and Mandalay was retaken.

Concerned that his left flank lay 'in the air' following the halting of the NCAC and the withdrawal by Chiang Kai-shek of its Chinese component, Slim instructed Major General Rees to rectify the situation. Consequntly, with 19 Indian Division safely across the Irrawaddy, on 6 March Rees pulled 62 Brigade out of the race for Mandalay and despatched it to Maymyo, 25 miles (40km) to the east. Using little more than smugglers trails the brigade advanced across two mountain ranges and a deep valley in four days, emerging to burst into the hill station to the complete surprise and consternation of the Japanese garrison there, many of whom fled north in a train that, to their great good fortune, happened to be standing in the station with steam up. The capture of Maymyo cut Japanese communications between the bulk of *Burma Area Army* on the central plain and detached units still facing the NCAC.

With 19 Indian Division in Mandalay and both 20 Indian Division and 2 British Divisions across the Irrawaddy around Myinmu, Kimura's northern front crumbled away, *15th Army* not so much retreating towards Meiktila as streaming south in disorganised groups, some large, some small, the army's effectiveness as a co-ordinated unit in danger of disappearing.

III

In The Arakan Lieutenant General Christison's XV Corps kept up the pressure on *28th Army* despite being shorn of its air transport. Demonstrating once more an ability to press into service that which would have been rapidly discarded in any other theatre than Burma, XV Corps amassed some 600 river and landing craft considered too 'clapped out' to be shipped to Europe, and with the support of both the Royal and Indian Navies engaged in a number of sea-borne outflanking manoeuvres, tense and dangerous under-takings, particularly among the swamps and chaungs of the southern Arakan coast.

By continually harassing and outflanking their Japanese opponents XV Corps pressed forward, capturing the strategically important town of Kangaw at the end of January and forcing a wedge between the two halves of *54th Division*, one half of which was located about An covering a road leading east over the hills, the remainder ensconced in strong defensive positions just north of Taungup, gateway to the Prome road. Here the Japanese had chosen well, for without transport aircraft to air-lift supplies to out-flanking columns advancing through the jungle, Christison would be reduced to a narrow frontal assault, and the futility of such attacks was well known.

Pressure had to be maintained, however, for Kimura had the bulk of *55th Division* in and around Prome ready to move on Meiktila. To prevent such an occurrence Christison was obliged to make a strong demonstration, however his problems encompassed not just the terrain and the Japanese but the fact that, so stretched were the air and ground forces attempting to keep 14th Army supplied, it became necessary to withdraw 81 Division and the bulk of 50 Tank Brigade from XV Corps to ease the difficulty.

Undeterred, in early February Christison despatched 82 West African Division, less one brigade, by boat along the Dalet Chaung to approach the pass about An from the north-west. Secondly he landed a brigade of 26 Division near Ru-ywa, some 30 miles (48km) south of Kangaw and 12 miles west of An. Supported by naval forces and a battery of medium artillery Ru-ywa was captured, but on the following day subjected to fierce counter attack that was only repelled with difficulty. Christison reinforced 26 Division and the encirclement of An was in progress when logistics finally got the better of XV Corps. An lay in some of the most impenetrable jungle hill country to be found in the Arakan and the advancing troops could only be supplied by air. With the battles at Mandalay and Meiktila at their height this was simply not possible and the advance ground to a halt.

Behind the Taungup position, Sakurai, the *28th Army* commander, was able to regroup the remainder of his Arakan garrison and despatch much of it across the Irrawaddy to join the attack on IV Corps in and around Meiktila.

Perhaps the principal contribution of XV Corps to the campaign, and a crucial contribution at that, was the capture of Akyab, Cheduba and Ramree islands which contained airfields and were, to a greater or lesser degree, accessible by sea, making them invaluable bases from which to transport supplies and equipment to 14th Army as it advanced first to Meiktila and then on to Rangoon.

Putting the all-weather airfields back into operable condition was a first priority but would take time, and it seemed that they might not be ready until May. This would coincide with the onset of monsoon and, in any event, would be too late to allow for the build up of supplies required for the southward thrust to Rangoon. As a consequence XV Corps engineers were obliged, simultaneously, to construct a number of fair-weather airstrips, much quicker to get into operation, which could be used in the meantime. This entailed a great deal of extra work, which nevertheless proceeded apace to the great relief of Lieutenant General Slim.

Chapter 6

Meiktila: The Defence

I

If the situation for XXXIII Corps in the north looked promising, it seemed less so for IV Corps. 28 East African Brigade around Chauk were subjected to fierce attempts to dislodge them, and, finally awoken to the threat to to his line of communications, Kimura ordered forces under the command of Major General Yamamoto, located to the south of Nyaungu, to step up their attempts to drive the 7 Indian Division bridgehead back into the river and isolate 17 Division at Meiktila.

Documents subsequently captured gave the Japanese plan as:

The *187th Independent Battalion* to occupy Kawton, 20 miles west of Ywathit and protect the Japanese left flank. The whole of *153rd Regiment*, known as the Left Column to advance to Myitche via Ledaing. One battalion of the *61st Regiment*, known as the Centre Column, to advance northwards from Singu, one battalion from the same regiment, known as the Right Column, to advance northwards from the Tetma area, the ultimate objective of the centre and right columns being Nyaungu.[45]

The attack opened 12 March with a company of Japanese troops storming a forward position in the village of Milaungbya held by elements of 4 Battalion 8 Gurkha Rifles, who subsequently withdrew. The Japanese Right column opened its offensive on the night of 15 March, a group of some 100 infantry emerging from the gloom to attack a company of 1 Battalion 11 Sikh near Tetma. The attack was beaten off but in all these engagements the Japanese proved highly adept at camouflaging their artillery, which then laid down an accurate harassing fire.

Patrols sent forward by 4/8 Gurkha to Milaungbya reported that the area appeared to be the object of a substantial Japanese build-up, the village itself being used as a firm base and gun area. Following up this information a company of 4/8 Gurkha launched an attack on the morning of 18 March supported by air strikes and a squadron of armoured cars. A sharp fight developed but by 1530 hours the Gurkhas had cleared the village. On their withdrawal, however, Japanese troops immediately reoccupied the area and on 20 March two companies of Gurkhas returned supported by air strikes, artillery fire, and tanks. Driven out once more, the Japanese did not reappear again in strength.

Lieutenant General Messervy had three distinct objectives for 7 Division:

1. To capture Myingyan. Until this was in Allied hands as a river-head 14th Army would be unable to utilise the Chindwin/Irrawaddy Rivers to relieve the strain on communications.
2. To open the road to Meiktila, closed by Japanese attacks.
3. To prevent increasing enemy pressure on both banks of the Irrawaddy from closing the road again.

Bitter, close-quarter engagements continued around the bridgehead, but 7 Division were not to be moved and by 18 March, against determined resistance, had elements pushed out as far as Myingyan. Much hard fighting remained but by 22 March the town was in 7 Division hands, and work began immediately on the construction of wharves to receive supply boats coming down from Kalewa on the Chindwin. 14th Army engineers also began work to resurrect the Myingyan/Meiktila railway, bridges were rebuilt, and even one or two wrecked locomotives were put into some semblance of order.

With the 7 Division operation to take Myingyan still in progress, Lieutenant General Naka, commanding the attempt to recapture Meiktila, made strenuous but, by force of circumstance, uncoordinated attacks on the town from the north and west. Not having the luxury of being able to await the arrival of *49th Division* from the south he used what he had, principally his own *18th Division* and the units despatched from *15th Army* by Kimura (see page 69).

Naka deployed *Sakuma Force*, plus *56th Infantry Regiment*, *18th Mountain Artillery* and the *12th Engineer Regiment* astride the Myingyan/Meiktila road to the south-west of the town, his line stretching around the southern perimeter to the south-east to effect a link with *49th Division* approaching from that direction and concentrating the remainder of his force to the north.[46] At this point 17 Division were outnumbered by Japanese forces swirling around the town, and dug in for what was going to be a hard fight. The question for the Japanese commanders was would they be able to coordinate their attacks to take maximum advantage of their present numerical superiority?

Appreciating the need for an experienced senior commander on the ground to bring some sort of order at Meiktila, and acutely aware of the overwhelming need to recapture the town, on 14 March Kimura issued the following order:

1. The *33rd Army* commander is placed in command of the battle at Meiktila. In the Lashio area, the *56th Division* commander will assume command of the *Otari Group* composed of the *56th Division*, elements of the *18th Division* and other rear units and will hold the enemy forces on the Shan Plateau, covering the right flank of the *15th* and *33rd* Armies.

2. The *33rd Army* commander, with only his headquarters, will proceed to Yamato Village, a suburb of Kalaw, to take command of the following groups and to destroy the enemy invading Meiktila: *18th Division* (less *114th Infantry Regiment* and one artillery battalion); *53rd Division* (less *128th Infantry Regiment*); and the *Sakuma Force* of the *33rd Division*. Communications and supply units will be assigned at a later date.

3. Transfer of command will be effective 0001 hours, 18 March.

4. The *15th Army* commander will command the *15th Division*; *33rd Division* (less the *Sakuma Force*), and the *Aoba Detachment* of the *2nd Division*. He will check the enemy invading the left bank of the Irrawaddy River so as to facilitate the operations of the *33rd Army* at Meiktila.[47]

By this order Lieutenant General Honda found himself and his *33rd Army* headquarters transferred from Lashio, in the north eastern sector opposite Sultan's emasculated NCAC and the now largely acquiescent Chinese, to Meiktila, where he was to attempt to retrieve the disastrous situation that had developed there.

At Yamato village on 17 March, Honda received his first appreciation of the situation from an officer just returned from a twenty-day tour of observation along the *15th Army* front facing XXXIII Corps.

The report was not optimistic. *15th Army* was reduced to one third its original strength, substantial losses had been incurred in artillery and other essential equipment, and the High Command, unaware of the losses, issued orders to divisions that they were simply unable to carry out. Morale was low. The continued resistance of *Burma Area Army* rested on the recapture of Meiktila; with that achieved and the crucial flow of supplies resumed it might be possible to hold on. If Meiktila could not be recaptured, the fate of the Japanese in Burma was sealed.

Honda issued his first orders to his new command 18 March:

1. I, the *33rd Army* Commander, commanding the *18th*, *49th* and *53rd Divisions* will destroy the enemy invading the vicinity of Meiktila.
2. The *18th Division* will secure the present line north of Meiktila. It will intercept and destroy enemy tank units and neutralise enemy airfields.
3. The *49th Division* will use its major strength to attack the enemy along the Pyawbe-Meiktila road and will occupy enemy positions in eastern Meiktila.
4. The *53rd Division* will withdraw immediately from its present line, through the area west of Meiktila, and will re-group its forces in the vicinity of Pyawbe.
5. I, the *33rd Army* commander, will leave for the Army Head-quarters at Hlaingdet on the morning of the 19th.[48]

Having been appraised of the parlous state of *15th Army*, whether in his heart Honda was as bullish as his order suggests is open to question, but he still expected the soldiers under his command to fight to the last and die for the Emperor rather than surrender. They would not disappoint him.

With units of *15th Army* streaming south toward Meiktila it is noticeable that his orders include the moving of *53rd Division* from north of the town around to Pyawbe, which lay astride his line of retreat south-eastwards to Rangoon. A prudent military decision, but not always of a type associated with Japanese commanders.

II

Honda was a capable, experienced commander and his efforts to dislodge 7 Indian Division encompassed not just the eastern bank of the Irrawaddy but also the west. Here the 28 East African Brigade position around Letse was to all intents and purposes besieged, and the subject of attack on an almost nightly basis from 4 March onwards. The standard Japanese tactic was to send forward small 'jitter' parties armed with grenades and small arms to infiltrate the defences in an attempt to create alarm and confusion.[49] Occasionally these nuisance raids would develop into something more serious as on the night of 19/20 March when Honda ordered an attack in battalion strength, supported by artillery and mortar fire, to coincide with similar advances on the east bank.

Gaining initial success the assault at Letse overwhelmed a platoon position and penetrated some 200 yards inside the defences, to be repelled by counter attack from 71 KAR and driven out at bayonet point by 4/14 Punjab, then under the East Africans command. This affair cost the defence 40 killed and 114 wounded, while 251 Japanese dead were counted, 2 prisoners captured, and a number of machine guns, documents and other equipment taken.

4/14 Punjab were also involved in an attack on the nearby 'Kidney' feature, a high point heavily defended by the Japanese. The raid achieved some success but the position proved too strongly defended to be taken at that time and the Punjabis withdrew to await a more opportune moment. Some days later a Punjabi patrol walked in on the Japanese while they were having tea, took a good look and still unnoticed turned around and left, taking an unattended light machine gun with them. This was judged to be the moment and a two platoon attack, supported by artillery, went rapidly forward. 'Kidney' was captured but a party of forty Japanese, having been driven off the feature, elected to set up a medium machine gun in full view on the flat open ground below. Engaged by the Punjabi mortar platoon the gun was destroyed and thirty-nine Japanese killed, the only survivor blowing himself up with a hand grenade.

Attack and counter attack continued in the area but the East Africans, like 7 Division, were not to be moved.

III

Major General Cowan's intention for the holding of Meiktila was offensive defence. 99 Brigade would hold the town itself while the remainder of 17 Division conducted offensive operations in strength to disrupt both Japanese attacks and any attempts by enemy units to slip past and retreat south.

As part of this strategy, on 8 March a detachment comprising two companies of 9 Border accompanied by the tanks of 9 Horse (minus two squadrons), a troop of 16 Cavalry armoured cars, one battery of 21 Mountain Regiment guns, a unit of 36 Field Squadron and an RAF VCP were despatched from Meiktila south along the Pyawbe road. It was believed that a strong force of Japanese with a 75mm gun had established themselves north of Pyawbe.

Advancing south-eastwards, the detachment flushed Japanese forces from several villages along the road, setting buildings afire, taking and inflicting casualties, and having one armoured car knocked out. Pushing on towards Pyawbe, on 9 March many more Japanese were encountered, believed to total battalion strength, with a further battalion in the town itself. Some 100 Japanese were encountered in the village of Yindaw and attacked by a company of 9 Border supported by tanks and mortar fire. Tank gun fire set the village alight and the Japanese scattered, leaving numerous casualties.

On 10 March the detachment returned to Meiktila leaving 'Spedforce', commanded by Lieutenant Colonel Spedding and consisting of 9 Border infantry, one squadron of 9 Horse tanks, one troop 82 Anti-Tank Regiment, one battery of 21 Mountain Regiment, and one platoon medium machine guns, as a forward bastion at Yindaw. 'Spedforce' remained in position for two more days, patrolling vigorously, obtaining much useful intelligence and discovering large dumps of Japanese clothing and ammunition.[50]

Some of the troops that the 17 Division detachment engaged were almost certainly advance elements of the upcoming *49th Division*. Some way ahead of the Division proper, the *Komatsubara Unit*, a specialised raiding party of some 500 men, were tasked with the recapture of the airfield east of Meiktila, making their attempt on the night of 14 March. The operation, however, was hastily and poorly planned, uncoordinated, recklessly executed, and a complete failure – the remnants of the *Komatsubara Unit* thereafter joining *18 Division*.

Much more troublesome to the airfield were Japanese 105mm guns, well hidden as usual, which accurately shelled the western end of the strip on the morning of the 15th, hitting a number of aircraft and causing a temporary halt to landings, supplies having instead to be parachuted in. Tanks scouring the pagoda area to the north of the town in response discovered and dealt with one of the guns.

Airfields, principally Thabutkon and that a couple of miles to the east of the town, were of prime importance as, despite the failure of Japanese attempts to dislodge the 7 Division bridgehead on the Irrawaddy, they had succeeded in cutting the road between there and Meiktila, leaving air supply the only way to replenish and reinforce 17 Division. Lieutenant General Slim now began to draw on 5 Indian Division, the fly-in of the airborne brigade of that division, 9 Indian Infantry, being completed in one day, 17 March, despite the airstrip being under direct artillery fire – a superb achievement by the British and American airmen involved.

Shortly after the arrival of 9 Indian Infantry, 17 Division found themselves virtually cut off from support as, with great effort and tremendous courage, attacking Japanese succeeded in closing both airstrips. Parachute drops continued but wounded could not be evacuated, supplies were greatly reduced, petrol ran short and reinforcement became impossible. At this critical juncture Major General Cowan also received news of a personal tragedy – his son had died of wounds received during the battle for Mandalay.

The airstrip at the eastern edge of Meiktila now became the focus of attention, it being the most conveniently placed for the flying in of all that 17 Division found themselves increasingly in need of. Having been driven off 15 March, Japanese forces returned to occupy a number of nearby villages on the night of the 18th and on the morning of the 19th began an accurate harassing fire on the southern end of the strip. Operations were undertaken to dislodge them but they remained stubbornly in place.

During this period a foray in strength was sent to sweep the area to the north in an attempt to discover and silence enemy artillery that had proved so effective in shelling the airfield. Leaving at first light 17 March, preceded by a divisional artillery bombardment, 63 Brigade (less 9 Border) supported by two squadrons of 5 Horse tanks, moved north encountering increasing opposition from the *15th* and *119th* regiments of *18 Division* as it went. By mid day the force was just south of the Mahlang road, having lost two tanks to artillery fire.

Pushing northwards, 63 Brigade engaged in a fierce fire fight during which Japanese 105mm guns were seen withdrawing from the area of the Myindawgan Lake to the north west. Tanks set off in pursuit, while an artillery Forward Observation Officer (FOO) directed fire on the retreating enemy from a self-propelled gun battery located on the west shore of Meiktila South Lake.

The sweep continued 18 March and was combined with an attack launched by 99 Brigade designed to catch enemy forces in the jaws of a pincer. At the close of the operation 63 Brigade withdrew having destroyed two enemy 105mm guns, four 47mm anti-tank guns, two medium machine guns, two medium tanks, four tractors and much equipment. Some 350 Japanese were known casualties, although many more were probably inflicted by artillery fire and air strikes. 63 Brigade suffered fifty-two killed or wounded.[51] In all operations such as this, air strikes would be much in evidence, swooping Allied fighter-bombers at times attacking enemy positions no more than 100 yards in front of friendly ground forces.

Furious strike and counter-strike continued unabated around the entire perimeter of the town and surrounding areas as the Japanese, thrown in piecemeal as they arrived, made increasingly desperate attempts to wrest control from 17 Indian Division. A significant element in the difficulty that Japanese commanders experienced in coordinating attacks rested with the poor state of communications between units. Radio traffic between *49th Division*, now in place to the south and east of the town, and *18th Division* to the north had to be routed through Army headquarters, and as a consequence were frequently delayed, interrupted, and garbled. This adversely affected mutual cooperation, an instance being the attack by the *Komatsubara Unit* on the east airfield. *18th Division* knew nothing of the attack until *Komatsubara* survivors straggled into their lines, and as a result were unable to provide any kind of support.

On the morning of 23 March *18th Division* launched its *55th* and *119th Infantry Regiments* on yet another attempt to capture the east airfield, making good progress until it became necessary to withdraw *55 Regiment* to cover the Meiktila/Thasi road, whereupon *119 Regiment* found it impossible to hold against repeated tank and infantry counter attacks supported from the air. Of increasing concern to Slim and other Allied commanders, however, was the fact that Meiktila appeared to be in danger of becoming a graveyard for vital transport aircraft, already in critically short supply. A further two were destroyed on the ground in this attack.

For Lieutenant General Honda, a considerable and continuing problem was to be the location of his headquarters. 14th Army HQ at Monywa had for some time been the beneficiary of a highly efficient wireless interception unit, capable of the accurate identification and location of enemy headquarters. With the invaluable assistance of aerial reconnaissance and informers even some of the most important, such as Honda's, were picked up and attacked time and again from the air, and on the ground if the opportunity presented itself. Consequently, since his arrival at Hlaingdet Honda's HQ had been subjected to intense bombing, the village destroyed, and he and his staff reduced to directing operations from foxholes in the surrounding jungle. Accordingly, he decided to move *33rd Army* HQ to Thasi, on the right flank of *49th Division*, from where he hoped to bring some coordination to operations. The move was made on the 25th.

With all the pressure on and around the airfields the supply situation for 17 Division was not good. Flights able to land were, by force of circumstance, intermittent, with such supplies that did arrive being more often than not dropped by parachute, however, for the Japanese outside the town things had deteriorated much farther. With 17 Division firmly across road and rail communications from Rangoon, essential large scale reinforcement and the supply of food, ammunition, and equipment of all kinds became impossible. By late March *18th Division* had lost half its artillery weapons and *49th Division* practically all of theirs, an estimated twenty guns remaining to *33rd Army* as a whole. Total casualties were of the order of 5,000,[52] while farther north, the predicament that *15th Army* found itself in was, if anything, worse. *Burma Area Army* was in the process of being choked out of existence.

On the night of 28 March Lieutenant General Tanaka, *Burma Area Army* Chief of Staff visited Honda at Thasi for an appreciation of the situation, which Honda gave him without pulling any punches. *33rd Army*, he said, would stand and fight to the last man if so ordered, but the plain fact was that it did not have the manpower or equipment to overcome 17 Division. The news that Tanaka brought was equally gloomy. *15th Army* was in full retreat before the rapidly advancing XXXIII Corps, and therefore, on his own authority, without consulting Kimura, the Chief of Staff instructed Honda that rather than attempt to recapture Meiktila the task for *33rd Army was* now a holding operation to cover the withdrawal of *15th Army*.

Honda issued orders accordingly:

1. The *15th Army* is retreating east from the area south of Mandalay toward the plateau east of Tozon. Its withdrawal is being covered by *33rd Division* which is under strong enemy pressure.
2. The *33rd Army* will facilitate the withdrawal of the *15th Army* by securing the present line extending from the north east to the south side of Meiktila.

   (NB: the 'present line' referred to actually involved *18th Division* moving 2–3 miles to the east and relinquishing the area north-west of Meiktila to 17 Division – see 3 below).
3. Breaking contact with the enemy on the night of 29 March, the *18th Division* will secure the vicinity of Thasi with its main body and the western sector of Hlaingdet with an element, in order to prevent the enemy moving eastward. Efforts will be exerted to neutralise the Meiktila airfields. The *Sakuma Force* will advance, without delay, to the Yozon area where it will revert to the command of *33rd Division*.[53]
4. The *49th Division* will secure its present line and check the enemy advancing southward.
5. The *53rd Division*, after assembling its troops in the sector west of Pyawbe, will secure the area surrounding Yanaung.[54]

IV

Airfields still featured in Honda's orders, and also played a great part in Major General Cowan's plans, the east airfield in particular, which lay just beyond the village of Kyigon. As a preliminary step to clearing the area, on the morning of 25 March 48 Brigade, less 1 Battalion 7 Gurkha Rifles, supported by a divisional artillery barrage and accompanied by one squadron of 5 Horse tanks, advanced on Kyigon and a copse 1,000 yards (914m) south of the village.

1 West Yorks were ordered to clear both points and advanced on a two company front, one company for the village one for the copse,

the latter held in some strength by infantry and artillery. Both companies were held up by artillery and mortar fire and Japanese infantry in bunkered positions, despite which a company of 4 Frontier Force Regiment and the tanks moved in on Kyigon, the advance proceeding slowly as the 5 Horse armour rumbled through the village blasting bunkers one by one. By 16.30 hours Kyigon was clear, but the copse remained in Japanese hands.

The following day 48 Brigade continued their advance, the intention being to complete clearance of the airstrip. The Brigade advanced in two columns preceded by an air strike on the copse, which, however, failed to silence enemy artillery secreted there. Immediately following the air strike two companies of 1/7 Gurkha Rifles, supported by two troops of tanks, made another attempt to take the area but were halted by heavy shell and mortar fire.

In the meantime, 4 Frontier Force Regiment, accompanied by two troops of tanks, circumvented the copse and approached the north end of the airstrip, coming under fire from a 70mm gun. A brisk fire fight developed but Japanese forces clung grimly on for another day.

27 March saw 4 Frontier Force Regiment renew its attack with tank support, this time on an enemy position south of the airstrip which was overcome. The airfield contained two runways, an east and a west strip, and a sweep of both now began, 1/7 Gurkha Rifles supported by two troops of tanks on the east strip, and a troop of tanks on the west strip. Heavy opposition was encountered from enemy infantry in bunkered positions and progress was slow, and while the airfield was eventually cleared, Japanese units remained in the vicinity.

Although at the time it probably did not seem like it to the troops on the ground, the brutal and bloody battles for control of Meiktila were drawing to a close. Coinciding with Honda's instructions to draw his *18th Division* to the north-east of the town, on 28 March, 63 Brigade, although unaware of the Japanese move about to get under way, launched a further attack towards the Myindawgan Lake area from the west and north-west, supported by 99 Brigade advancing from Meiktila, both with tank support.

Preceded by heavy bombing that was, however, not properly coordinated and not entirely successful, 63 Brigade began its advance behind a heavy screen of forward patrols, encountering stiff opposition from a 'rabbit warren' of bunkered positions and slit trenches. A number of ammunition dumps were discovered and destroyed by tank and artillery fire as the brigade moved forward. Numerous Japanese were discovered occupying a strong point well located in difficult tank country flanked by the lake and with a number of nullas to provide cover from air attack. To circumvent this obstacle a squadron of 5 Horse tanks supported by a company of 7 Baluch fought its way across the Pindale road north of the lake, encountering mines which damaged one tank. Continuing the destruction of ammunition and supply dumps, by 1600 hours the squadron had cleared the area north and east of the lake while elsewhere 5 Horse tanks discovered and neutralised Japanese artillery. Moving south along the Mahleng Road 1 Battalion 10 Gurkha Rifles encountered Japanese guns and infantry located on high rough ground unsuitable for tanks. These enemy units proved particularly difficult to dislodge even when subjected to 'earthquake' bombing assault, and a decision was taken that for the time being the Gurkhas should go around and isolate the position rather than attempt to go over it.

Attacking north west across the road linking Meiktila with Mandalay, 99 Brigade pressed forward, 6 Battalion 15 Punjab plus 1 Battalion 3 Gurkha Rifles attacking the sluice area at the western end of the lake preceded by heavy air attack and concentrated artillery fire. One platoon managed to get across the sluice but there the attack stalled, both battalions pinned down by machine gun fire from well dug in bunkered positions. Concentrations of artillery fire were called down and the battalions tried again, once more to no avail. Casualties were heavy, ninety-two including one company commander.

18 Division, offering fierce resistance but squeezed in a pincer movement between the two 17 Indian Division Brigades and responding to Honda's order, slowly gave ground to the north and east, 1/3 Gurkha Rifles together with 6/15 Punjab sweeping north in response to link up with 7/10 Baluch. Elaborate bunker positions were discovered in the newly captured area, some capable of holding 400–500 men.

By 29 March the encirclement of Meiktila was over, although it would not be until the 31st that the area around the airstrip would be clear enough to allow aircraft to land once more.

Chapter 7

Rangoon and the Final Battles

I

Attacked by 63 Brigade from the west and 99 Brigade advancing from Meiktila, *18th Division* was obliged to withdraw to the north east before being able to swing around to the south east to take up defensive positions around Thasi. On 29 March Honda moved his headquarters to Nyaungyan, strategically placed between his *18th* and *49th Divisions*, but away from the Meiktila/Thasi road so that attack by armoured units was unlikely, although it was still open to air strike. On 1 April just such an attack destroyed Honda's headquarters building, staff officers barely escaping with their lives and the *33rd Army* commander finding himself buried up to his waist in rubble, although escaping serious injury.

The attack on Honda's HQ at Nyaungyan was but a small example of what Lieutenant General Slim now had to put into operation along the whole front. He had to keep Kimura, his commanders, and their troops off balance and in a continuing state of short term 'crisis management' while he organised his own forces for the dash to Rangoon. And 'dash' it would be for there existed the fear that if Rangoon could not be taken quickly Kimura might have time to organise a suicide garrison, such as that which had just been encountered at Meiktila, to defend the the town and its invaluable port facilities until the onset of monsoon. This course of events would leave 14th Army stranded at the end of an exceptionally long line of communications, with large scale air supply at best a severe problem in the appalling weather to be encountered and well nigh impossible without the USAAF squadrons due to be withdrawn on 1 June. A nightmare scenario such as this might well result in withdrawal back to Meiktila, possibly farther, and the need to take on a reorganised, replenished, and reinforced *Burma Area Army* when monsoon finally blew itself out.

Two lines of approach to Rangoon were possible – (1) along the railway line from Meiktila, and (2) farther to the west, down the valley of the Irrawaddy. While one route would have to take precedence for logistical reasons, the intention was in fact to use both, with a full corps and a tank brigade on each to keep Kimura's already disjointed forces split between two fronts.

Initial planning for this phase had in fact begun at 14th Army HQ the previous July, detailed planning being undertaken with the establishment of bridgeheads over the Chindwin in November. In large measure the problem facing Slim and his planning staff came down to the terrain to be encountered. On leaving Meiktila the open tankable country of the Central Plain would be left behind and, on either line of approach, the troops would be confined to a single road from which it would be difficult to deploy in dry weather let alone the impending monsoon. This would necessitate fast armoured columns punching their way through to Rangoon, while inevitably leaving behind sizeable enemy contingents to roam the countryside, the objective being to secure the port first then turn around to deal with any opposition that remained.

Lieutenant General Slim selected the railway axis for his principal advance, this being the shorter of the two by some 50 miles (80km) and also the more straightforward. The farther south along the Irrawaddy valley that troops progressed the more chaungs, large and small, there were to be encountered, many of which could be crossed only by bridges, most of which the Japanese would have blown as they withdrew.

IV Corps had under command two air transportable divisions, 5 and 17 Indian, was already concentrated around Meiktila and was therefore selected for the southward push along the railway while XXXIII Corps, some 50 miles to the north, would be required to undertake a complex sweep across IV Corps lines of communication from the north-east to the south-west in order to reach the Irrawaddy Valley. The movement would be made on a broad front across the central plain to effect the clearance of any remaining opposition from the south and south west of Mandalay. On reaching the Irrawaddy the corps would commence its advance south along the river valley. In view of the fact that 5 Indian Division was newly arrived and fully equipped, 7 Indian Division was transferred to XXXIII Corps.

While speed in the capture of Rangoon was the principal objective of the coming manoeuvres, Slim's instinctive desire to destroy the enemy's ability to wage war was also drawn into the equation. Without sacrificing any of the rapidity of movement required, the jaws of the IV Corps/XXXIII Corps pincer would trap *28th Army*, what remained of *15th Army* and elements of *33rd Army* in malarial swamps and the trackless jungle of the Pegu Yomas during monsoon and cut them off from supplies and their only means of escape – retreat eastwards to the safety of Siam (now Thailand).

An essential feature of the rapid advance would be the close cooperation of the air forces in the form of both fighter-bombers for ground support and transport aircraft for the essential supply of the fast-moving forward echelons. In this the services of the USAAF would be essential not only in the area of transport aircraft, but in the provision of air transportable engineer battalions, for which the RAF had no equivalent. These units would be flown to landing areas hacked out of the jungle by 14th Army engineers just behind the front line, and would then have the task of turning these crude airstrips into runways suitable for fighters and transports in double-quick time while the army moved rapidly on.

II

Operation 'Dracula', the proposed amphibious assault to capture Rangoon, had an on-off career and was, for the most part, opposed by Generals Slim and Leese since the troops for it would have to come from 14th Army, and both initially felt that, at full strength, that army could take the port unaided. Their advice was accepted, and subsequently, as the supply of troops eased somewhat, Operation 'Roger', a landing by the newly formed XXXIV Corps in the area of Phuket, on the Kra Isthmus, entered detailed planning as a precursor to the recapture of the Malaysian Peninsular and Singapore.

However, having witnessed the desperate time-consuming defence of Meiktila that the Japanese were able to mount, towards the end of March both Slim and Leese had a change of heart and General Leese proposed to Mountbatten the shelving, for the time being, of Operation 'Roger', and using the troops thus released for a modified 'Dracula', since the consequences for 14th Army of not taking Rangoon by monsoon could be catastrophic, and would negate any benefits gained by a landing at Phuket.

Reinstatement of 'Dracula' at such a late stage would take what Mountbatten termed 'heroic' measures, however a special meeting of the relevant Commanders-in-Chief was arranged for 2 April at Kandy to discuss the prospects. At that meeting Leese and Air Chief Marshal Sir Keith Park, Allied Air C-in-C, agreed that if exceptional efforts were made the required land and air forces could be made available. Significant problems, however, attended the naval aspect of the operation and Admiral Sir Arthur Power, C-in-C East Indies Fleet, reminded those present that the launching of an amphibious assault after the first week in May would be an exceptionally hazardous undertaking. The bases from which 'Dracula' would be launched were Akyab, by sea approximately 480 miles (772km) from Rangoon, and Kyaukpyu approximately 430 miles (692km) distant.

Given the possible consequences of not reviving 'Dracula' Admiral Power proved willing to accept the risks involved, and Mounbatten therefore authorised an emergency amphibious assault by one infantry division supported by armour and a composite battalion of airborne troops, such landings to be undertaken not later than 5 May with provision for reinforcement by an additional infantry division should it become necessary.

Air Chief Marshal Park considered that the destruction of Japanese defences on Elephant Point, guarding the seaward approaches to Rangoon, would be impossible by bombing alone, consequently one parachute battalion was assigned the task, to be flown in by two transport squadrons which would, by force of circumstance, have to be withdrawn from 14th Army airlift operations for the purpose.

III

IV Corps had two immediate tasks, to consolidate its position around Meiktila preparatory to making its movement south, while simultaneously maintaining pressure on its Japanese opponents to prevent them from regrouping. 19 Indian Division would remain in the Central Plain to complete clearance of the area Mandalay/ Thasi/Meiktila and secure lines of communication, while IV Corps struck out for Pyawbe, 30 miles (48km) south east of Meiktila, led by 99 Brigade, 17 Indian Division.

Initial objectives for IV Corps were the capture of Pyinmana and, farther south, Toungoo, for their airfields. *49th Division*, however, offered fierce resistance, notably at Yindaw. Ordered to bypass the village 17 Division pressed on to toward Pyawbe, while Yindaw was reduced by 5 Division and the air forces following a three-day battle in which the defenders were practically wiped out.

Lieutenant General Honda, meanwhile, moved his headquarters once again – to Pyawbe. Barely established in a garage on the outskirts of the town[55] Honda was startled by an outbreak of heavy firing and glanced out to see IV Corps tanks heading straight for him. Lying flat as the building came under fire the *33rd Army* commander began writing his will, but at the last moment the tanks veered off and once again he escaped serious injury.

Pyawbe presented a good natural defensive position and Honda rapidly drew together what remained of *18 Division*, *49 Division* and the bulk of *53 Division* – a total of around 5,000 men. This defence put up the usual stubborn, diehard performance, but a coordinated series of attacks by 17 Division, the air forces, and a decisive thrust by 255 Indian Tank Brigade saw what remained of Honda's *33rd Army* scattered, and with it any chance the Japanese might have had of opposing IV Corps in strength.

Pyawbe fell to 17 Division 10 April and the following day 5 Indian Division, preceded by an armoured column, passed through 17 Division to take up the advance. The armoured column moved quickly through Yamethin the same day, but infantry and the division transport vehicles were held up by a Japanese force of some 300 men equipped with anti tank guns which infiltrated the village between the passing of the armoured column and the arrival of the rest of 5 Division. These Japanese infantry were assisted by a rare appearance from the Japanese Army Air Force which sent over four fighters, in all probability Nakajima Ki-43 Oscars, which destroyed a number of vehicles carrying fuel for the armoured column; however two of the enemy aircraft were shot down, infantry cleared the town, and 5 Division pressed on.

As has been mentioned the air forces followed close behind the rapidly advancing front line, leapfrogging airstrips being required every 50 miles, closer if possible. Ronald White, an armourer with 152 Squadron, recalled that one night a ragged Japanese soldier crawled into the squadron camp. White was convinced that he just wanted to surrender, but he was shot anyway.[56] The Japanese had created for themselves a fearsome reputation, and now they paid the price. Few prisoners were taken during 14th Army's headlong rush to Rangoon.

On 16 April 5 Division captured Shwemyo, some 240 miles (386km) from Rangoon, and Honda decided on a withdrawal to Pyinmanma, issuing the following order:

1. The Army will check the southward advance of the enemy by securing the area around Pyinmana.
2. The *18th Division* will break contact with the enemy this evening, 16 April, and will check the southward advance of the enemy by occupying the area from the Sinthe River bridge, east of Pyinmana, to the uplands to the east.
3. The *53rd Division* will withdraw along both sides of the railway to Pyinmana to secure the immediate vicinity of Pyinmana in cooperation with the *55th Division*. The *Tanaka Heavy Artillery Battalion* (two 105mm guns) will be dispatched to Pyinmana where it will come under the command of *53rd Division*.
4. The *55th Division* will also secure the vicinity of Pyinmana.
5. The *49th Division* will concentrate its strength at the rear of the *18th Division*.
6. Army Staff Officers will give instructions at Pyinmana concerning it's defence by the *53rd* and *55th* Divisions.
7. I will depart for Pyinmana at midnight on 16 April.[57]

Honda's order got through to all his divisions with the exception of the *49th*, and by the morning of 18 April the *18th* and *53rd Divisions* had reached the line designated and were beginning the construction of defensive positions. Japanese estimates put the strength of these divisions at this time at no more than 4,000 men for the *18th* plus two 105mm guns and three mountain guns, while the *53rd* was able to muster around 3,000 men plus the *Tanaka Heavy Artillery Battalion*.

Honda and Staff Officers Tsuji, Tanaka, and Kibino were on hand from the morning of 17 April, Honda establishing his command post of some 300 personnel in a small village 2 miles south of Pyinmana, from where they oversaw the positioning of the divisions mentioned plus the *55th* which arrived in echelons and by the morning of the 19th numbered around 1,500 men plus four mountain guns. Realising that the scratch force of which he now had command could not hope to hold for long, Honda reported his situation to *Burma Area Army* requesting permission to arrange his forces in a series of defensive positions in depth, enabling him to conduct a successive series of holding actions. On the morning of the 19th Kimura peremptorily telegraphed back that *33rd Army* was to continue to hold north of Pyinmana.

Lieutenant General Honda had already experienced a number of narrow escapes but what followed was the narrowest. By nightfall on the 18th the *33rd Army* command post had been established around a temple in the jungle 2 miles south of Pyinmana, connecting lines of trenches being dug for guard units while other personnel occupied one-man foxholes dug among the trees (see diagram on p. 97). One covered position capable of withstanding mountain artillery shelling was constructed for Honda and his staff.

On the morning of 19 April, preceded by air attacks, armoured units leading 5 Indian Division pushed toward Pyinmana in two columns, one along the main road, one along the railway. One column then swung around the town in an attempt to gain the airfield beyond at Lewe, and en route attacked the headquarters position, an estimated twenty tanks overrunning Sector II by 0830 hours. Supported by infantry and more tanks resistance was soon crushed, Honda and his staff taking refuge in the temple. Luck was again with the *33rd Army* commander, however, as the airfield at Lewe was the prime objective and the 5 Division armoured column moved on, although the area was from time to time sub-jected to heavy bombing. At one point Honda peeked out from the temple to see Indian stretcher bearers moving about, one stopping to pick up a wounded Japanese officer and carry him away. Prior to the destruction of the Radio Section Kimura managed to get one message through, which read: 'To Commander *33rd Army*. You will hold the line from Toungoo to Pyinmana'.[58] The *Burma Area Army* Commander had apparently not been appraised of or did not believe the disasters that had befallen *33rd Army*.

After dark Honda, accompanied by some 150 headquarters staff, and assisting a further 100 wounded, left the village and moved north, Honda surmising that the roads to the south would be closely watched. Infiltrating 5 Division lines, the small party moved east to

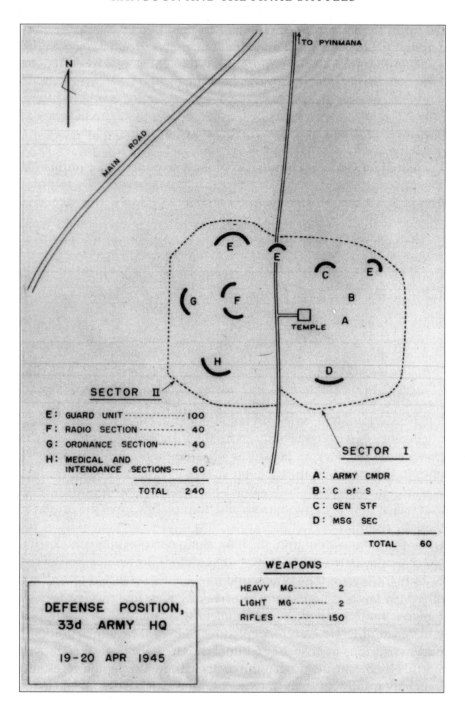

the railway and from there moved south, passing once more through 5 Division lines and finally arriving at a village 6 miles south of Pyinmana on the morning of the 20th.[59]

In 14th Army attention now focused on the next major objective. The airfields grouped around Toungoo were regarded as some of the best in Burma and were, crucially, within fighter range of Rangoon, enabling the air forces to provide essential cover for 'Dracula'. With the amphibious assault now scheduled for 2 May, realistically Toungoo had to be taken by 25 April at the latest.

Kimura also appreciated the significance of Toungoo and made desperate attempts to drive such forces that he still had in the Shan Hills toward the town. Both sides hustled their men on in what developed into a race, the principal road by which the Japanese travelled being a fair weather hill track that ran parallel to the route taken by IV Corps, but 60 miles to the east. Some 70 miles from Toungoo the track taken by the Japanese turned abruptly westward and joined the Rangoon road in the town.

For a time it looked as though Kimura might win the race but Slim still had an ace to play. Led by the partly reorganised *15th Division* the Japanese route south led them through Karen territory. The Karens, one of several tribes indigenous to Burma, remained staunchly loyal to the British through the darkest days of the Japanese occupation, and suffered as a result. For some time British intelligence had been in contact with the tribe through Force 136, the clandestine military organisation that operated behind Japanese lines in Burma. Over time a good sized force, the Karen Guerrillas, was armed, equipped and trained for just such an opportunity as that which now presented itself, and Slim readily gave the order for them to rise up.

For the Japanese column, pushing along narrow jungle tracks, the effect was as dramatic as it was unexpected. Previously hampered by only the terrain they now found themselves subjected to ambush on a daily basis, bridges were blown along their line of advance and foraging parties killed. British officers with the Karens, equipped with ground-to-air radio, drew down air strikes which inflicted many casualties and destroyed vital motorised transport.[60]

With their rate of progress much reduced the Japanese fought their way grimly forward until they reached Mawchi, some 50 miles east of Toungoo. Here their advance was stalled for several days by a relentless series of Karen ambushes, road blocks, and demolitions.

Kimura had lost the race, but there were Japanese forces in Toungoo, principally disorganised elements of Honda's *33rd Army*, including the army commander. Nevertheless when IV Corps tanks burst into the town 22 April – three days ahead of schedule – so great was the surprise that a Japanese military policeman remained on point duty and was shot down as the tanks roamed the streets hunting his compatriots. Once again Honda himself escaped, this time forced to leave behind most of what remained of his head-quarters equipment, and it what some time before he managed to regain any semblance of control over his rapidly disintegrating army.

IV Corps now had 160 miles (257km) to go and eight days in which to reach Rangoon. In addition to the more serious reasons for hurrying, a certain competitive element also entered the race between IV Corps and XV Corps (the latter earmarked to make the amphibious landing), as to which would actually capture the port. At this stage betting at 14th Army Headquarters was three to one on IV Corps, tempered by a feeling that a '31st April' on the calendar would be helpful.

IV

While IV Corps pushed down the line of the railway, farther west and following the Irrawaddy, XXXIII Corps also pressed its advance. In fear of having their escape route to Siam cut by IV Corps, large numbers of General Sakurai's *28th Army* attempted to escape to the east using a road from Taungdwingyi across the Pegu Yomas, the town also controlling the strategically important main road running southward down the east bank of the Irrawaddy to Allanmyo and Prome. On 13 April the Japanese garrison was taken completely by surprise when 20 Indian Division burst in on them and captured the town against slight resistance. So unexpected was the attack and so fragmented were Japanese communications at this stage that for days after its capture enemy convoys continued to pour in on their way east, only to receive a suitably warm recep-tion. 20 Division then pushed west to capture Myingun and Magwe on 19 April.

Farther north the battle-hardened 7 Indian Division advanced astride the river, good progress being made along the west bank while units on the east bank found themselves held up by determined Japanese resistance at Kyaukpadaung. The town lay on the main route between Chauk and Meiktila and was an important railhead for a branch line connecting the Mandalay–Rangoon railway with Pyinmana.

Kyaukpadaung fell 12 April and with it 7 Indian Division secured their left flank and rear and pressed on toward the highly prized oilfields around Yenangyaung. Japanese resistance was spasmodic, but when encountered it was, as usual, determined. Nevertheless by 21 April Yenangyaung was surrounded and on 22 April 7 Division completed its capture.

On 28 April Allanmyo fell, followed 2 May by Prome, the important river port and eastern terminus of the road from Taungup. These manoeuvres trapped large numbers of Japanese in the Pegu Yomas and cut the last escape route for Sakurai's *28th Army* in the Arakan

V

IV Corps, meanwhile, continued its rapid advance and the day following the capture of Toungoo 5 Division made 30 miles (48km) to Pyu. Here an important bridge had been demolished but the town was not defended and construction of a Bailey bridge was soon in hand. At this time the 3,000 men of the 1st Division of the Indian National Army were encountered but the division surrendered enmasse and were put to work on captured airfields.

17 Indian Division readied itself to take the lead, but 5 Division would have none of it and pressed on a further 20 miles (32km) to Penwegon. Here the Japanese prepared another important bridge for demolition and as the lead 5 Division armoured car crept forward the demolition party were discovered on the bridge – asleep. Their sleep proved to be a long one.[61] IV Corps was now 114 miles (183km) from Rangoon.

Kimura's options were few indeed. *33rd Army* had been destroyed at Meiktila and was to all intents and purposes no longer a coherent fighting force, its commander, Honda, a fugitive. The destruction of *15th Army*, begun at Imphal and Kohima, was completed at Meiktila, and what remained of Sakurai's *28th Army* was bottled up in the Arakan and the Pegu Yomas. Terauchi, the Japanese Supreme Commander, far away from the realities of the battle front, ordered Kimura to hold southern Burma, including Rangoon, at all costs, but Kimura concentrated what forces he could at Pegu. These comprised *24 Independent Mixed Brigade* from Rangoon plus a miscellaneous collection of troops amounting to approximately two further brigades with a number of anti aircraft guns for use in an anti tank role. Pegu, located on the Mandalay–Rangoon railway some 80 miles north east of Rangoon, represented the last remaining escape route to the east and relative safety in Siam.

17 Division, preceded by 255 Indian Tank Brigade, took over the lead and pressed forward, all IV Corps troops now on reduced rations having sacrificed food for gasoline, such was the limited amount of aircraft space available and so vital the need to keep the spearhead moving. Inevitably Japanese units roaming around in rear caused problems, in particular at Toungoo where elements of *15 Division* equipped with artillery dug in and shelled the area, causing casualties. In reserve for just such incidents as this, 19 Indian Division advanced and with the assistance of Mitchell bombers, and guerrillas to infiltrate and pinpoint enemy positions, drove the enemy eastward and away from the airfields.

By 26 April 17 Indian Division was at Daik-U, 85 miles (136km) from Rangoon. Briefly delayed by Japanese suicide squads near the Moyingyi reservoir, by 29 April advance units of 255 Tank Brigade were entering the outskirts of Pegu, while a second armoured column headed south-eastwards to cut the Japanese line of retreat to the Sittang and Siam. This, however, was where luck deserted 14th Army, for on that same day the heavens opened and torrential monsoon rains lashed Pegu and many areas of Burma. IV Corps slithered to a halt, roads hitherto blanketed by chocking dust transformed into rivers axle deep in mud. Forward airstrips were washed out and useless, 221 Group having no option but to withdraw all save one of its close-support squadrons from Toungoo. To effect some measure of air cover Thunderbolt P-47s were flown at maximum range from central Burma supported by two Mitchell bomber squadrons of the 12th US Bombardment group, which found themselves given the unusual task of providing direct support for advancing ground troops.

Towards the end of April Slim established his headquarters at Meiktila and it was there, on the 29th, that he learned of the renewed Japanese activity at Toungoo. At that time 19 Indian Division had only a single brigade in reserve to counter this attack and Slim took the decision to fly down the following day to assess the situation for himself. Driving from the airfield to Rees HQ Lieutenant General Slim observed for himself Japanese artillery shelling the road.

Rees himself seemed sanguine enough and assisted by the Karens, who harassed the Japanese unmercifully, was able to keep the line of communications open. While at Toungoo reports of the battle at Pegu came through and Slim determined to fly down to take a look for himself, accompanied by General Messervy and several others including Major Robert Fullerton, a US Army officer on the 14th Army Staff.

Flying over Pegu Slim instigated what he later described as a 'very foolish and culpable act'.[62] Wishing to see what manner of countryside 17 Division would encounter beyond Pegu, and observing tall columns of smoke from the direction of Rangoon, he told the pilot to fly on south. The aircraft came under sustained and accurate anti-aircraft fire and received several hits, one of which exploded against Major Fullerton's leg. Showing great skill and presence of mind the pilot took evasive action and landed the aircraft at a newly constructed advance strip just north of Pegu, where, as fortune would have it, John Bruce, 14th Army consulting surgeon, happened to be visiting a forward surgical team.

One of Britain's leading surgeons, Bruce was able to save Major Fullerton's life, but at the unavoidable cost of the injured leg. With an honesty unusual in those of high rank – inside or outside the army – Slim later castigated himself for the error, recognising that putting himself as Army Commander, plus General Messervy and the others at high risk, was neither advisable or necessary.

Operation 'Dracula', in the meantime, was in motion. Force W, commanded by Rear Admiral Martin formed up into six convoys, plus a carrier force to provide air cover, and made ready to leave Akyab and Kyaukpyu, the slowest convoy 27 April for Rangoon, the remainder following three days thereafter.

It looked very much as though XV Corps would win the race to liberate the port, but in fact Rangoon was liberated by the RAF.

On 1 May two pathfinder aircraft and thirty-eight transports of the 317th and 319th Troop Carrier Squadrons USAAF lifted off from Akyab carrying Gurkha paratroops which they successfully dropped without incident over Elephant Point. The following day Dakotas of Nos 194 and 267 Squadrons RAF dropped rations and ammunition.

That same day, 2 May, Wing Commander Saunders, Officer Commanding 110 Squadron RAF, took his Mosquito on a low level reconnaissance mission over Rangoon in response to a report from a similar flight the previous day which mentioned what appeared to be lettering on the rooftops at Rangoon jail. Flying low over the prison Saunders observed two messages: 'Japs gone British here, and the second, somewhat more succinct, 'Extract digit'.

Rather than report back, Saunders landed his aircraft at Mingaladon, one of the Rangoon airfields, hitch-hiked to the jail and released a number of prisoners of war. Having achieved the single-handed capture of the capital and principal port in Burma, Saunders borrowed a native boat, rowed down river to meet the incoming invasion force and informed them that Rangoon was undefended, which came as something of a shock – albeit a pleasant one.

IV

The capture of Rangoon did not end the campaign for, while Kimura's forces were scattered and defeated, they were not prepared to surrender and showed every inclination of trying to attempt a break out eastwards across the Sittang and into Siam. Intelligence reports showed the Japanese to be gathered for the most part in four distinct areas:

1. The Irrawaddy Valley. Here, on both banks of the river *28th Army* had, north of Prome, *54th Division* with units of the *49th* and *55th Divisions*, what was left of *72 Independent Brigade* and *2 Indian National Army Division*. Farther south, mainly in the hills of the Pegu Yomas, were parts of *55th Division* and a considerable body of line of communication troops, total strength estimated at 15,000 men and all engaged in trekking east to cross the Meiktila–Rangoon road and join with friendly forces east of the Sittang.

2. The Shan Hills east of Meiktila. Making their way south were *56th Division* and remnants of the *15th, 18th* and *53rd Divisions*, about 6,000 in all.
3. East of the Sittang River opposite the 14th Army cordon from Toungoo to Nyaunglebin. Remains of *33rd Army* containing a hotch-potch of units from the *2nd, 18th, 49th, 53rd,* and *55th Divisions*, and, farther east in the Salween Valley, the battered *31st* and *33rd Divisions* with large numbers of line of communication troops. Total estimated 25,000 men.
4. In the area Mokpalin-Moulmein east of the mouth of the Sittang and on the east coast of the Gulf of Martaban. Here Kimura collected around him *24 Independent Brigade*, the evacuated Rangoon garrison, survivors from the Pegu battle and various line of communication units, total estimated strength 24,000 troops.[63]

Various smaller bands of stragglers roaming the country and not included in these groupings were believed to bring estimates of the total number of the enemy still at large to approximately 70,000 men – a figure later discovered to be a substantial under-estimation. Slim was determined that these disparate groupings should not be allowed to concentrate east of the Sittang where they might again become a thorn in the side and delay projected operations for the recapture of Malaya. Accordingly the following orders were issued to IV Corps:

- Destroy all enemy attempting to cross the Pegu Yomas from west to east.
- Take Mokpalin.
- Advance with 19 Division, which now reverted to IV Corps, as far as Thaudaung, 20 miles east of Toungoo and secure 14th Army line of communications.

To XXXIII Corps, operating in the Irrawaddy Valley:

- Destroy all enemy in the Irrawaddy Valley.
- Open the road and railway from Prome to Rangoon.
- Capture Bassein.

The security of Rangoon and its environs was entrusted to 26 Division, which was also to establish a link with 20 Division south of Prome.

For the Japanese their principal concern was for the west bank of the Irrawaddy where Lieutenant General Sakurai had much of the *54th Division*, which appeared to be in reasonable order, plus Yamamoto Force, comprising approximately seven battalions with artillery, in total around 10,000 men. Sakurai organised his command into two groups, Yamamoto Force to the north to delay 7 Division, while *54th Division* attempted to cross the river farther south and gain relative safety in the Pegu Yomas. On the east bank of the river were the badly used-up *55th Division* plus *2 Indian National Army Division.*

XXXIII Corps engaged in a number of minor skirmishes as it pushed farther south, but on 11 May bumped into Yamamoto Force in strongly prepared positions about 35 miles (56km) north-west of Allanmyo. In a battle lasting four days 7 Division destroyed the Japanese rearguard, the remains of which streamed south for Kama, a village on the river some 20 miles (32km) above Prome where *54th Division* were already making their way across and had formed a bridgehead on the bank opposite. *72 Independent Brigade* had already crossed here and escaped into the Pegu Yomas.

7 Division approached along both banks of the river, completing the destruction of Yamamoto Force on the west bank, and encircling the bridgehead on the east bank. *54th Division* made numerous furious and fanatically determined attempts to break through the cordon with great loss and little success. After the battle 1,400 Japanese bodies were counted, but many more undoubtedly lay undiscovered in the jungle. Small parties did manage to escape through to the hills but *54th Division* essentially ceased to exist, having lost not only much of its manpower but all its transport and artillery.

The bulk of what remained of the Japanese forces were now penned up in the Pegu Yomas. With monsoon at its height, ceaseless rain, every chaung in full flow, little shelter and without military or medical supplies, they faced a bleak future dying of exposure, disease, and malnutrition. In an attempt to avoid further loss of life allied aircraft dropped leaflets inviting surrender and promising good treatment, over the areas in which this wretched 'army' banded together but with no response. Given, therefore, that they would not lay down their arms they were obliged at some point to try to break out eastwards across the Mandalay–Rangoon Road in an attempt to rejoin what remained of Kimura's forces across the Sittang River.

The 14th Army, although undoubtedly in better shape than the Japanese, also suffered privations due to the withdrawal of the USAAF transport squadrons on 1 June and the transfer of several RAF squadrons from Burma to take part in the build up to the impending Malaya campaign.

In a spate of command changes Lieutenant General Slim was chosen to succeed Leese as Allied Land Forces Commander, his place at 14th Army being temporarily filled by Lieutenant General Christison until his permanent replacement, Lieutenant General Sir Miles Dempsey, arrived in theatre. A new army, the 12th, was formed under Lieutenant General Stopford to continue land operation in Burma, the intention being for 14th Army to participate in Malaya. Many veterans of the Burma campaign would remain, however, as IV Corps (now under Lieutenant General F.I.S. Tuker, Messervy being on leave), comprising 5, 17, and 19 Indian Divisions, plus 255 Indian Tank Brigade transferred to 12th Army, which also retained under command 7 and 20 Indian Divisions, 82 West African Division, 22 East African Brigade, and the Burma National Army, renamed the Patriotic Burmese Forces (PBF), under its charismatic leader Aung San. Headquarters XXXIII Corps ended its distinguished career, being disbanded to form the nucleus of the new HQ 12 Army.

General Slim had not seen home for 7 years, and, given the opportunity for leave, he took it. While he was in the UK the final battle of the Burma Campaign, variously called the Battle of the Sittang Bend, or The Battle of the Break-Out, was fought.

Sakurai managed to form his 'army' into five groups:

1. *54th Division* farthest north.
2. *72 Independent Mixed Brigade.*
3. *28th Army HQ* with various units and line of communication troops.
4. *55th Division*, less approximately one brigade.
5. *105 Independent Mixed Brigade.*

Stopford's 12th Army was disposed along the Rangoon–Mandalay Road masking escape routes exiting the Pegu Yomas from Hlegu to Pyinmana, with 7 Division farthest south, 17 Division in the centre, and 19 Division farthest north. Sakurai's options being few in number Stopford had a good general idea of what he would do, and these suppositions were confirmed when, on 2 July, a long distance patrol from 17 Division captured a *55 Division* order that gave the Japanese plan in detail. Sakurai proposed, with his forces disposed in several columns, to break out across the Mandalay–Rangoon Road on a front of some 150 miles (241km) between Toungoo and Nyaunglebin. The routes to be taken (all in the 17 and 19 Division sectors) and the forces allotted to them were contained in the order, all that was missing was the date.

Forewarned of Sakurai's intentions, Stopford drew in substantial reinforcements and arranged his defences in depth facing the proposed routes that the Japanese would take. Patrols were pushed deep into the hills along these tracks to give early warning, and strong points with artillery and armour established where the Japanese would emerge from the hills to the road. Dispersed across the plain that led to the Sittang, columns of infantry awaited any who managed to get that far. Along the west bank of the Sittang yet more regular battalions and PBF units lay in wait for those that attempted to get across, and on the east bank patrols from Force 136 and more PBF units lay in wait to ambush survivors who managed to get that far.

The briefest glance back through the pages of history will confirm the futile waste of life that political, military, and religious fanaticism have inflicted upon the human race. What followed was one more example.

In an attempt to divert attention from Sakurai's break-out, *33rd Army*, numbering around 6,000 men on both banks of the Sittang, attacked 7 Division positions in an attempt to cut 12th Army communications with Rangoon and convince Stopford to move reinforcements south and out of the 17 and 19 Division areas. The fighting was fierce, the battlefield a swamp in which any sort of movement was conducted only with the greatest difficulty. Finally the attacks, which went on for days, were broken up with the help of RAF fighter bombers and the attempt failed with substantial loss to both sides.

The failure of the diversion notwithstanding, commencing 19 July Sakurai's attempted break-out began. Some 100 Japanese attacked a 17 Division platoon post, followed piecemeal in both the 17 and 19 Division sectors by groups of up to 500 or 600 men who would debouch piecemeal from the Yomas to attack the nearest defence post, usually with great loss. Survivors shattered into smaller groups to press on eastwards across the plain where they were hunted down by infantry columns, strafed by aircraft of the RAF and Indian Air Force, and stalked by PBF and Burmese irregulars, men with long memories and bitter scores to settle.

Those that arrived at the Sittang found the river in monsoon flood. Launching makeshift rafts, logs, anything that would float, they tried to get across, most of those not shot in the attempt being swept helplessly away on the rapid current to drown. Down river a 7 Division post counted over 600 Japanese bodies floating by from the tragedy unfolding upstream.

Last to run the gauntlet were *12* and *13 Naval Guard Forces*, men of the Imperial Japanese Navy Port and Shore Establishments. Amounting to some 1,200 men, they chose to make their attempt last and alone. On 31 July this meagre force battled across the road suffering numerous casualties, and struggling across the plain arrived at the Sittang to find their way blocked by one battalion while another closed in from behind. With the country flooded it took a week for one Indian and one Gurkha battalion to overcome the sailors, Japanese sources later stating that only three of their number survived.

Japanese losses suffered during the course of the break-out are difficult to assess. Over 6,000 bodies were recovered by 12th Army, many hundreds more claimed by the PBF and other Burmese irregulars, while many more must have lain undiscovered in the water and long grass. Japanese sources later confirmed that less than 6,000 starved, exhausted and diseased survivors reached the east bank of the Sittang.

Sakurai abandoned between 1,000 and 2,000 of his men, those too weak and sick to march, to die in the Pegu Yomas.

Against an estimated 12,000 Japanese killed 12th Army losses were 95 dead, 350 wounded. IV Corps reported that that they had taken 740 prisoners, an unheard of ratio – ten times higher than previously experienced – but if realisation as to the futility of continuing the struggle had begun to dawn it was all much too late.

On 6 August 1945 the first atomic bomb destroyed Hiroshima and on 9 August the second obliterated Nagasaki. Six days later a message broadcast by Emperor Hirohito to the Japanese population stated that they must 'bear the unbearable' and surrender unconditionally. For many in the Japanese homeland this was the first negative war news they had received from their political leaders in 4 years.

Notes

1. A Chinese 'army' approximated the strength of a European Corps, containing two or three divisions of some 3,000 rifles per division at full strength, also light and medium machine guns, but no artillery with the exception of an occasional light anti-tank gun. A Japanese 'army' would also correspond to the size of a European Corps but would be better trained and equipped than its Chinese equivalent, particularly with regard to artillery.
2. Slim, First Viscount William, *Defeat into Victory*, Cassell, 1956, p. 118.
3. TNA Air 41/37, *Air Supply Operations in Burma 1942–1945*, p. 4.
4. Moore, Major J.H., Royal Australian Infantry, *Japanese Command Crisis in Burma 1944*.
5. For greater detail on the air war see Pearson, Michael, *The Burma Air Campaign 1941–1945*, Pen & Sword, 2006.
6. Swinson, Arthur, *Four Samurai*, Hutchinson, 1968, p. 148.
7. *Japanese Monograph No.148*, Burma Area Operations Record.
8. *Ibid.*, note 2, pp. 357–8.
9. *Ibid.*, note 2, pp 373–4.
10. Air Chief Marshal Sir Keith Park, when C-in-C Allied Air Forces SEAC, called the Ledo Road 'the longest white elephant in the world'. Started in December 1942, the road was not completed until January 1945 and was of limited strategic or supply value, despite taking 17,000 Allied engineers and approximately US$148,000,000 to build.
11. *Japanese Monograph No. 148*, Burma Area Operations Record, p. 163.
12. *Ibid.*, p. 164. Although according to Slim, *Defeat Into Victory*, p. 392, it was the *53rd Division* that Kimura transferred to *15th Army*.

13. P.N. Khera M.A., S.N. Prasad Ph.D., *Official History of the Indian Armed Forces in the Second World War 1939–45, Reconquest of Burma, Vol. II.* Combined Inter-Services Historical Section (India & Pakistan), 1959, p. 257.
14. The Lushai Brigade was a disparate collection of spare Indian battalions and local levies under the command of Brigadier Marindin, formed to prevent Japanese infiltration through the Lushai Hills. Despite little in the way of transport or equipment it performed very well, largely in the 'guerilla' role.
15. Slim, First Viscount William, *Defeat into Victory*, Cassell, 1956, p. 393.
16. Mountbatten, Vice Admiral The Earl, *Report to the Combined Chiefs of Staff by the Supreme Allied Commander South East Asia 1943–1945*, HMSO, 1951, pp. 121–2.
17. *Ibid.*, note 5, p. 400.
18. *Ibid.*, note 6, p. 107.
19. Lieutenant General Browning pioneered the development and use of airborne troops for the British Army. Closely involved with Market Garden in September 1944 he told Field Marshal Montgomery that, with regard to the Arnhem aspect of the operation, 'we might be going a bridge too far'.
20. At the instigation of Prittam Singh of the Indian Independence League and Major Iwaichi Fujiwara, the Indian National Army (INA) was formed in February 1942 from Indian Army prisoners of war captured by the Japanese. The INA failed militarily during the Second World War but was instrumental in helping to gain Indian independence from Britain in 1947.
21. *Ibid.*, note 13, p. 243.
22. The term 'Indian' or 'British' Division can be a little misleading as Indian Divisions would often include British units, and British Divisions would certainly include Indian units, particularly after the Normandy landings when the limited pool of British replacements and reinforcements remaining by 1944 tended to be sent to Europe as a mater of priority.
23. Second Lieutenant Imai's story is recounted at greater length and in his own words in *Tales of Japanese Soldiers*, Kazuo Tamayama and John Nunnelly, Cassell, 2001, pp. 216–21.
24. Slim, First Viscount William, *Defeat into Victory*, Cassell, 1956, p. 417.

25. *Ibid.*, pp. 425–6.
26. TNA WO 172/6975, p. ii.
27. *Ibid.*, note 2, p. 282.
28. *Ibid.*, note 26, p. ii.
29. *Ibid.*, note 2, pp. 438–9.
30. TNA WO 172/7147.
31. *Ibid.*, note 1, p. 289.
32. Mountbatten, Vice-Admiral The Earl, *Report to the Combined Chiefs of Staff by the Supreme Commander South-East Asia 1943–1945*, HMSO, 1951, pp 134–5.
33. Swinson, Arthur, *Four Samurai*, Hutchinson, 1968, pp. 178–9.
34. TNA WO 172/6986. 17 Indian Division intelligence appreciation put together from captured Japanese documentation and prisoner of war interrogation.
35. TNA WO 172/7147.
36. Slim, First Viscount William, *Defeat into Victory*, Cassell, 1956, pp. 446–7.
37. *Ibid.*, note 13, pp. 298–9.
38. *Ibid.*, note 3, p. 11.
39. *Ibid.*, note 5, pp. 300–1.
40. *Ibid.*, note 5, p. 302 and note 2, p. 12.
41. *Japanese Monograph No. 148*, Burma Area Operations Record, 33rd Army Defence Operations April 1944–August 1945, pp. 168–9.
42. Hill, Major John, MC, c/o 'B' Company, *China Dragons: A Rifle Company at War, Burma 1944–1945*, Blandford, 1991, pp. 107–8.
43. The long knife with curved blade widening toward the tip favoured by the Gurkhas.
44. *Op. cit.*, note 2, pp. 116–18.
45. IV Corps Operations Instruction No. 135, quoted in *Official History of the Indian Armed Forces in the Second World War 1939–45, Reconquest of Burma, Vol. II*, p. 317.
46. *Japanese Monograph No. 148*, Burma Area Operations Record, 33rd Army Defence Operations April 1944–August 1945, p. 169.
47. *Ibid.*, p. 171.
48. *Ibid.*, p. 174.
49. *Op. cit.*, note 2, p. 334.
50. TNA WO 172/6986.
51. *Ibid.*, note 2, p. 174.

52. *Op. cit.*, note 2, p. 177.
53. Relations between *Burma Area Army* and the armies in the field had been under strain for some time and staff officers at Kimura's Headquarters strongly objected to the return of *Sakuma Force* to *33rd Division* as it would seriously weaken *33rd Army*, but Honda carried out the order despite their objections.
54. *Ibid.*, p. 178.
55. Swinson, Arthur, *Four Samurai*, Hutchinson, 1968, p. 181.
56. Ronald White. Conversation with the author.
57. *Japanese Monograph No. 148*, p. 189.
58. *Op. cit.*, note 1, p. 184.
59. *Op. cit.*, note 3, p. 193.
60. Air strikes were vital for the destruction of Japanese motor transport. In the nine months leading up to the dash to Rangoon more than 3800 Japanese vehicles were destroyed from the air. Mountbatten, Vice-Admiral The Earl, *Report to the Combined Chiefs of Staff by the Supreme Allied Commander South-East Asia 1943–1945*, HMSO, 1951, footnote, p. 153.
61. Slim, First Viscount William, *Defeat into Victory*, p. 501.
62. *Ibid.*, p. 504.
63. *Ibid.*, p. 510.

Appendix I

IV Corps Order of Battle, February 1945

Corps Headquarters
HQ Corps Artillery, Engineers etc.

Artillery
67 Heavy AA Regiment HQ
187/188/189 Heavy AA batteries
28 Light AA Regiment HQ
106/112/250 Light AA batteries
8 Medium Regiment HQ
246/247 Medium Batteries
1 Br Svy Regiment
B Flight 656 Air Operations Squadron RAF

Engineers
471 CAG Engineers
CRE IV Corps Engineers IE
75 Indian Field Company IE
2 Faridkot Field Company ISF
424 Ind Field Company IE
305 Ind Field Pk Company IE
12 Engineer Battalion IE
725 Mechanical Equipment Platoon IE

Signals
HQ IV Corps Signals
IV Corps Artillery Signals Section
210 Ind Signals Monitoring Section
IV Corps Cipher Section
471 CAG Engineers Signals Section

67 Heavy AA Regiment Signals Detachment
28 Light AA Signals Detachment
8 Medium Regiment Signals Detachment

Infantry
78 Ind Infantry Company

Royal Indian Army Service Corps
HQ CRIASC Corps Troops
103/127/238 Ind Companies
21/28/55/59 Ind MA Platoons
6/14/15 Ind Field Ambulance Troop Cl. 1
332 Ind Supply Section (under command IV Corps Forward Airfield
  Maintenance Organisation (FAMO))
45 T. Company (M)
6/47/48 Ind Companies
54 Ind Local Purchase Section
8 Ind Field Bakery Section

Medical
14/19 CCS
3 Ind Mobile X-Ray Unit
4/9 Ind Mobile FT Units
8/14 Ind Mobile Surgical Units
65 Ind Field Ambulance
50 Ind Field Hvg section
5 Ind Bearer Company
45 Sub Depot Medical Stores
32/68 Ind Anti-Malaria Units
17/19/30/68 Ind Dental Units (IT)
45/49/53/80 Ind Dental Units (BT)
10/19/20/23 Ind Dental Mechanical Units
3/89 Ind Staging Sections
4 Platoon American Field Service MAS
5/32 Field Transport Units
85 Mobile X-Ray Unit
Psychiatric Centre
11 Ind Ophthalmic Unit
9 Ind Field Laboratory

Ord
HQ IV Corps Ord Field Park
IV Corps and Army Troops Ord Sub Park
7 Indian Division Ord Sub Park
17 Indian Division Ord Sub Park
No. 1 Mobile Ammunition Inspection Unit
No. 1 Mobile Ammunition Laboratory Unit
11 Ind Ord (Mobile Laundry & Bath Unit)
13 Ind Mobile Bath Unit

REME/IEME
HQ CIEME Corps Troops
551/555 Indian Infantry Troop Workshops (B)
70 Mobile Workshop Company (less 1 section)
100 Ind Mobile Workshop Company
329/338 Lines of Communication Reconnaissance Companies
67 Heavy AA Regiment Workshop Section
28 Light AA Regiment Workshop Section
8 Medium Regiment LAD (B)
3 Ind Telecom Repair Team
IV Corps Signals LAD (B)
305 Ind Field Park Company LAD
103/109/127/238 Indian Transport Company Field Workshop
    Sections
96 Ind Transport Workshop Section

Pro
HQ IV Corps Pro Unit

Int
573 FS Section
3 FIC
2 Mobile Section CSDIC
6 Pl BIC
14 Pl BIC (less one section)

Postal
HQ IV Corps Postal Unit (less detachment and FPO H-273)
FPO H-390 & H-449

Canteens
28 CBID

Indian Pioneer Corps
1360/1397/1440/1468 Companies IPC

Misc
51 Ind Company D
No. 4 & 5 Control Centre Forward Maintenance Area
B Group V Ops (temporarily attached)
4 Section Sea Reconnaissance Unit
Small Boat Section

7 INDIAN DIVISION

HQ 7 Indian Division
HQ 7 Indian Division Pro Unit
568 FS Section

Artillery
HQ 7 Indian Division Royal Artillery
136 Field Regiment RA – RHQ
347/348/500 Field Batteries
139 Field Regiment R – RHQ
362/364/503 Field Batteries
24 Anti-Tank Regiment RA – RHQ
86/205/284 Anti-Tank Batteries
25 Ind Mountain Regiment – RHQ
5/23/BB Indian Mountain Batteries

Engineers
HQ 7 Ind Division Royal Engineers
62/77/421 Ind Field Companies
331 Ind Field Park
854 Heavy Bridging Platoon

Signals
HQ 7 Indian Division Signals
7 Indian Division Artillery Signals Section
33/89/114 Ind Infantry Brigade Signals Sections
136/139 Field Regiment Signals Sections
24 Anti-Tank Regiment Signals Detachment
25 Indian Mountain Regiment Signals Section

Infantry
7/2 Punjab (Divisional Reconnaissance Battalion)
13/13 Frontier Force Rifles (Medium Machine Gun Battalion)
2 Baroda HQ Battalion

33 Indian Infantry Brigade
Brigade HQ
4/15 Punjab
4/1 Gurkha Regiment
1 Burma Regiment

89 Indian Infantry Brigade
Brigade HQ
2 Kings Own Scottish Borderers
1/11 Sikh
4/8 Gurkha Regiment

114 Indian Infantry Brigade
Brigade HQ
2 South Lancashire Regiment
4/14 Punjab
4/5 Gurkha Regiment

RIASC
HQ RIASC
29/30/31/32 ICIS
5/20/63 Anti-Tank Companies (M)
65 Anti-Tank Company (Mixed)
60/61 GP Transport Companies
28 (East African) Brigade Op Company EA ASC

Medical
44/54/66 Ind Field Ambulance
32 Ind Field Hygiene Section

Ord
ADOS Dump
2 × Laundry Section 11 Mobile Laundry & Bath Units
2 × Bath Section 11 Mobile Laundry & Bath Units
Section 120 Ord Field Park

REME/IEME
HQ 7 Indian Division IEME
6 & 39 Indian Infantry Mobile Workshop Companies
7 Indian Division Reconnaissance Company
33/89/114 Ind Infantry Brigade LD Type I and detached workshop
60/61 Ind Division Transport Company Workshop Sections
24 Tank Workshop Section
133 Indian Infantry Workshop Company

Vet
7 Mobile Vet Section

Postal
33/89/114 Brigade detached divisional postal units

Formations temporarily under command 7 Indian Division:

28 EAST AFRICAN INFANTRY BRIGADE GROUP
HQ 28 (EA) Brigade

Engineers
63 (EA) Field Company

Signals
28 (EA) Brigade Signals Section

Infantry
7 (U) Kings African Rifles
46 (TT) KAR
71 (S) KAR
Chin Hills Battalion
Western Chin Levies
Lushai Scouts

RIASC
28 (EA) Brigade Op Company EA ASC

Medical
64 Indian Field Ambulance
108 CRS

Mechanical Engineers
28 (EA) Brigade LAD
9 IB Workshop Ssection

Pro
28 (EA) Brigade Pro Section

Postal
APO (EA) 82

17 INDIAN DIVISION

HQ 17 Indian Divisional
HQ 17 Indian Division Pro Unit
602 FS Section

Artillery
HQ 17 Indian Division Royal Artillery
129 Field Regiment RA – RHQ
311/312/493 Field Batteries
1 Indian Field Regiment Indian Artillery – RHQ
1/2 Indian Field Batteries
82 Anti-Tank Regiment RA – RHQ
87/228/276 Anti-Tank Batteries
21 Indian Mountain Regiment Indian Artillery – RHQ
1 (Royal) Mountain Battery
1 (Jacobs) Mountain Battery
37 Mountain Battery

Engineers
HQ 17 Indian Division Royal Engineers
60/70 Indian Field Companies
Tehri Gerhwel Company
414 Indian Field Park Company

Signals
HQ 17 Indian Division Signals
48/63/99 Indian Infantry Brigade Signals Sections
17 Indian Division Artillery Signals Section
129 Field Regiment Signals Section
1 Indian Field Regiment Signals Section
82 Anti-Tank Regiment Signals Section
21 Indian Mountain Regiment Signals Section

Infantry
6 Jat (Divisional Reconnaissance Battalion)
9 Frontier Force Rifles (Machine Gun Battalion)

6 Rajput (Divisional HQ Battalion)
48 Indian Infantry Brigade
Brigade HQ
1 W. Yorkshire Regiment
4 Frontier Force Rifles
1/7 Gurkha Rifles
63 Indian Infantry Brigade
Brigade HQ
9 Border Regiment
7 Baluchistan
1/10 Gurkha Rifles
99 Indian Infantry Brigade
Brigade HQ
6/15 Punjab Regiment
1 Sikh Light Infantry
1/3 Gurkha Rifles

RIASC
HQ RIASC
902/906 Companies RIASC
9/10/11/44 Comp Pl

Medical
23/37/50 Indian Field Ambulance
22 Indian Field Hygiene Section
91 Indian Anti-Malaria Unit

REME/IEME
HQ 17 Indian Division IEME
17 Indian Division Reconnaissance Company
1/59/123 Indian Infantry Mobile Workshop Companies
48/63/99 Indian Infantry Brigade LAD Type I
129 Field Regiment LAD Type B
1 Indian Field Regiment LAD Type B
82 Anti-Tank Regiment LAD Type B
21 Indian Mountain Regiment LAD Type III
9 Frontier Force MG Battalion LAD Type I
17 Indian Division Signals LAD Type II
414 Indian Field Park Company LAD Type II

902 Indian Company Workshop Section Type D
906 Indian Company Workshop Section Type C

Vet
4 Indian Mobile Veterinary Section

Postal
17 Indian Division Postal Unit

Misc.
57 Company D Force

14th Army troops and other units temporarily under command IV Corps:

255 INDIAN TANK BRIGADE GROUP
(Temporarily under command 17 Indian Division)
HQ 255 Indian Tank Brigade

RAC/IAC
5 Horse Group
116 Regiment RAC Group
3 Independent British Troop RAC less 3 sections
2 TDS (43 Cavalry)

Artillery
59/18 Field Battery Royal Artillery

Engineers
36 Indian Field Squadron IE

Signals
255 Indian Tank Brigade Signals Squadron
59/18 Field Battery Signals Section

Infantry
4/4 Bombay Grenadiers less 3 companies

RIASC
590 Company RASC (Tank Transporter) less 3 platoons
2 Ind Comp Pl
40 Indian Company IASC

Ord
255 Indian Tank Brigade Ord Field Park

REME/IEME
255 Indian Tank Brigade HQ IEME
255 Indian Indian Tank Brigade Workshop
42 Indian Tank Troop Workshop
1 Recovery Company
2 TDS Workshop Detachment
5 Horse Group LAD
116 Regiment RAC Group
9 Royal Horse Group

Artillery
2 Indian Field Regiment HQ
3/4/7 Indian Field Batteries
5 (M) Indian Anti Tank Regiment HQ
17/18/20 (M) Indian Anti Tank Batteries
1 Indian Light AA Regiment HQ
2/3/6 Indian LAA Batteries

Signals
2 Indian Field Regiment Signals Section
5 (M) Indian Anti Tank Regiment Signals Detachment
1 Indian LAA Regiment Signals Detachment

IEME
2 Indian Field Regiment Workshop Section
5 (M) Indian Anti Tank Regiment LAD
1 Indian LAA Regiment Workshop Section

28 (EAST AFRICAN) INFANTRY BRIGADE GROUP
HQ 28 (EA) Infantry Brigade

Engineers
68 (EA) Field Company

Signals
28 (EA) Brigade Signals Section

Infantry
7 (U) Kings African Rifles
46 (TT) Kings African Rifles
71 (S) Kings African Rifles

28 (EA) Brigade Def Pl
Western Chin Levies

RIASC
28 (EA) Brigade Op Company EA ASC

Medical
64 Indian Field Ambulance
108 CRS

ME
28 (EA) Brigade LAD
9 IB Workshop Section

Pro
28 (EA) Brigade Pro Section

Postal
APO (EA) 82

99 INDIAN INFANTRY BRIGADE GROUP
HQ 99 Indian Infantry Brigade

Artillery
87 Anti Tank Battery Royal Artillery
21 Indian Mountain Regiment RHQ
1 (Royal) Mountain Battery
1 (Jacobs) Mountain Battery
37 Mountain Battery

Engineers
Tehri Garwhal Company

Signals
99 Indian Infantry Brigade Signals Section
21 Indian Mountain Regiment Signals Section

Infantry
6/15 Punjab
1 Sikh Light Infantry
1/3 Gurkha Rifles
'D' Company 9 Field Force Rifles (MG Company)

RIASC
44 Indian Com Pl

Medical
50 Indian Field Ambulance

IEME
99 Indian Infantry Brigade LAD Type I

457 FORWARD AIRFIELD ENGINEERS GROUP
HQ Forward Airfield Engineers
24 Engineer Battalion IE
363/402 Indian Field Companies IE
751 ME Pl

IV CORPS FORWARD AIRFIELD MAINTENANCE ORGANISATION (FAMO)
HQ FAMO

Signals
45 Beach Group Signals Detachment

Ord
Section 45 Beach Group Ord Detachment

WESTCOL
Battalion HQ
Chin Hills Battalion
Lushai Scouts

Appendix II

XXXIII Indian Corps
Order of Battle

Corps Headquarters
HQ Corps Artillery, Engineers etc.

Headquarters XXXIII Indian Corps
HQ Royal Artillery, XXXIII Indian Corps
HQ XXXIII Indian Corps Emil. Pl.
3 & 201 S.W. Secs.

Artillery
1 Medium Regiment Signals Section & LAD
8 Medium Regiment less 1 Battery, Signals Section & LAD
67 Heavy AA Regiment & Workshop Section
69 & 78 Light AA Regiments & Workshop Sections
43/2 Svy Battery RA
44/2 Svy Battery RA
'D' Troop 44 Comp Svy Battery
1 (WA) HAA Battery
19/7 (Rajput) HAA Battery less one troop
CB Staff
3 Indian CB Tram.

Engineers
HQ XXXIII Indian Corps Troops Engineers
24/67/80/362/429 Indian Field Companies
332 Indian Field Park Company
1 Indian Division Br. Pl.
Suket Division Br. Pl.
10 (Pathan) Indian Engineer Bt.
HQ IV Corps Troop Engineers
75/94/424/428/ Indian Field Companies

305 Indian Field Park Company
XV Indian Div Br. Pl.

Signals
XXXIII Corps Signals
205 Indian Monitoring Section
241 W/T Section

Infantry
HQ Assam Zone V Force
1 Det. 3 V Force
1 Det 4 Assam Rifles
Burma Escort Company (Kabaw Valley Detachment)
Kabaw Detachment Burma Regiment
9 Jats Machine Gun Battalion
80 Indian Infantry Company, 14 Punjab.

S.T.
8 Motor Transport Regiment HQ
37/40/64/100/164 GPT Companies
904 & 905 Jeep Companies & Workshop Sections
HQ American Fields Services
1/2/3/4 MAS (AFS)
61 MAS
78 DID
312 & 550 Indian Supply Sections (POL)
328/339/495/544/628 Indian Supply Sections
54 & 75 AT Companies

Medical
13/16/26 Indian CCS
20/55/68/69 Anti-Malaria Units
33 & 44 Indian Anti-Malaria Units
3/10/82 Mobile X-Ray Units
5/9/10/14 Indian Mobile Surgical Units
56 Indian Field Hygiene Sections
7 Malarial Forward Treatment Unit (Dimapur)
8 Malarial Forward Treatment Unit (Kohima)
5 & 27 Field Transfusion Units
5 Bearer Company

67 & 76 Indian Staging Sections
64 & 67 Indian Field Ambulance
9 Indian Light Field Ambulance
17 & 19 Indian Dental Units
44 Indian Sub Depot Medical Stores
1/2/3/4 American Field Service Platoons

Pro
XXXIII Corps Pro Unit

Ord
19/23/36 Indian Ord Mobile Cinema Units
5 Indian Ord Mobile Laundry & Bath Unit
11 Indian Ord Salvage Unit
14 Salvage Unit
19 & 37 Indian Ord Salvage Units
HQ IV Corps OFP
IV Corps Troops & Army Troops Ord Sub Pk.
2 British Division Ord Sub Pk.
5 Indian Division Ord Sub Pk.
11 Division Ord Sub Pk.
17/20/23 Indian Division Ord Sub Pks.

Electrical & Mechanical Engineers
1 Infantry Troops Workshops
60/81/112 Indian Mobile Workshop Companies
328 & 333 Line of Communication Reconnaissance Companies
24 Indian Brigade RASC Workshop Pl.
1067 Indian GPT Workshop Section

Remount & Veterinarian
3 & 7 Indian Advance Remount Depots
10/15/18/20 Indian Field Remount Sections
3 Indian Saddle Fitting Team
10 Indian Field Vet Hospital
21/22/25 Indian Advance Field Hospitals
21 & 22 Indian Field Depot Vet Stores
1 & 15 Indian Mobile Vet Sections

Postal
48 Indian FPO

Int.
575/579/589/590/598 Indian FS Sections
3 Mobile Section SEATIC
2 & 3 Advance FIC
Der No.204 IFBU
51 Observation Squadron

Survey
AD Survey & Pz.
Detachment 6 Field Survey Company
33 Map Supply Section

P & L
1340/1466/1467/1488 Indian Pioneer Companies

Mess Companies
Nos 3/41/138/162/163/342/336/388 Mess Units
Nos 1/6/62 Sjts. Mess Units

Misc
25 AASC
115 PW Cage
'E' Graves Registration Unit
IV Corps Elephant Unit

254 INDIAN TANK BRIGADE

Headquarters
HQ 254 Indian Tank Brigade
254 Indian Tank Brigade HQ Squadron Tank Troop
149 RAC (less one squadron) and LAD
3 DG & LAD
3 Bombay Grenadiers & LAD

Engineers
401 Indian Field Squadron

Signals
254 Indian Tank Brigade Signals Squadron

S.T.
609 GPT Company
589 Tank Transporter Company

Medical
14 Indian Light Field Ambuloancs less one section

Pro
254 Indian Tank Brigade Pro Unit

Ord
104 Indian Ord Field Pk (Tank Brigade) less detachment
Detachment 105 Indian Ord Field Pk.

Electrical & Mechanical Engineers
Detachments 2 & 4 Tank Recovery Companies
Section 5 Indian Mobile Workshop Company
74 Indian Mobile Workshop Company
203 Mobile Wireless Workshop Section

Postal
63 Indian FPO

2 BRITISH DIVISION

Headquarters
HQ 2 Division
Royal Artillery 2 Division
Royal Engineers 2 Division
RASC 2 Division
REME 2 Division
Def. & Empl. Pl.

Armoured Corps
2 Reconnaissance Regiment Signals Section & LAD
11 Cavalry

Artillery
10/16/19 Field Regiments Signals Sections & LAD
100 AA/Anti Tank Regiment Signals Section & Workshop Section
(B) (less 2 AA batteries)

Engineers
5/208/506 Field Companies
21 Field Park Company & LAD (B)

Signals
2 Division Signals & LAD (A) (Less infantry brigade signals sections)

MG Battalion & Inf.
2 Manchester MG & LAD less 1 company

REME
2 Division Troops Workshop
4/5/6 Brigade Workshops

Medical
4/5/6 Field Ambulance
2 Field Hygiene Section
44 AM Unit

S.T.
8/24/29 Infantry Brigade Companies RASC
387 Div Tps RASC

Pro
2 Division Pro Unit

Postal
2 Div Postal Unit
131/132/133 Field PO

Int
1 Brit. FS Section

Infantry
4 Infantry Brigade
HQ 4 Infantry Brigade & Signals Section
HQ 4 Infantry Brigade Def Pl & LAD (A)
HQ 4 Infantry Brigade REME & LAD
1 Royal Scots
2 Norfolk
1/8 Lancashire Fusiliers
5 Infantry Brigade
HQ 5 Infantry Brigade & Signals Section
HQ 5 Infantry Brigade Def Pl & LAD (A)
HQ 5 Infantry Brigade REME & LAD
7 Worcester Regiment
2 Dorset
1 Cameron Highlanders
6 Infantry Brigade

HQ 6 Infantry Brigade & Signals Section
HQ 6 Infantry Brigade Def Pl & LAD (B)
HQ 6 Infantry Brigade REME & LAD
1 Royal Welch Fusiliers
1 Royal Berkshire
2 Durham Light Infantry

5 INDIAN DIVISION

Headquarters
Main HQ 5 Indian Division
Rear HQ 5 Indian Division
HQ Royal Artillery 5 Indian Division
HQ 5 Indian Division RE
HQ 5 Indian Division Signals
HQ 5 Indian Division Regiment RIASC
HQ 5 Indian Division Indian Electrical & Mechanical Engineers

Artillery
4 Field Regiment RA Signals Section & LAD
28 (J) Field Regiment RA Signals Section & LAD
56 AA/Anti Tank Regiment Signals Detachment & Workshop Section
24 Indian Maintenance Regiment Signals Section & LAD

Engineers
2/20/74 Indian Field Companies
44 Indian Field Park Company

Infantry
3/2 Punjab less three companies
HQ 9 Indian Infantry Brigade Signals Section & LAD (E)
2 West Yorkshire
3 Jat
3/14 Punjab
'D' Company 3/2 Punjab
HQ 123 Indian Infantry Brigade Signals Section & LAD (E)
2 Suffolk Regiment
2/1 Punjab
1 Dogra
'C' Company 3/2 Punjab

HQ 161 Indian Infantry Brigade Signals Section & LAD
4 Royal West Kent
1/1 Punjab
4 Rajput
'A' Company 3/2 Punjab

RIASC
238/239/240 IGPT Companies
7/60/61/62 Indian Company Issue Sections
23 AT Company (M)
60 Mule Company
66/74/82 AT Companies (M)
5/22/23 Indian Field Ambulance Troops Cl 1

Medical
10/45/75 Indian Field Ambulance
7 Indian Field Hygiene Section

Pro
3 Indian Division Pro Unit

IEME
113 Indian Mobile Workshop Company
5 Indian Recovery Company

Veterinarian
2 Indian Mobile Vet Section

Postal
21/22/23/169 Indian FPO

Int
565 FS Section

11 (EAST AFRICAN) DIVISION

Headquarters
HQ 11 Division
HQ RA 11 Division & Signals Section
HQ 11 Division RE., Signals Section & LAD
HQ 11 Division EAASC
HQ 11 Division RAEME
HQ 11 Division LAD

Artillery
302/303 Field Regiments EAA, Signals Sections & LAD
304 Anti Tank/Light AA Regiment & LAD

Engineers
54/58/64 Field Companies EAE
62 Field Park Company

Signals
11 Division Signals, Cipher Section & LAD

S.T.
1/2/3 Infantry Brigade Company
11 Division Tps Company

Medical
2 (Z) Field Ambulance
6 (U) Field Ambulance
10 Field Ambulance
71 Field Hygiene Section
60/61 FDS
2004 SB Company

Pro
11 Division Pro Company

EME
11 Division Army Tps Workshop
1/2/3 Infantry Brigade Workshops

Int
5 Fd S Section

Postal
11 Division Postal Unit

Misc
12 Observation Units
13 Fd Infs Pl.
11 Division Salvage Unit

Infantry
21 Infantry Brigade
HQ 21 Infantry Brigade

21 Infantry Brigade Signals Section Cipher Section & LAD
2 (NY) Battalion Kings African Rifles
4 (U) Battalion Kings African Rifles
1 Northern Rhodesia Regiment
25 Infantry Brigade
HQ 25 Infantry Brigade
25 Infantry Brigade Signals Section Cipher Section & LAD
11 (K) Battalion Kings African Rifles
26 (TT) Battalion Kings African Rifles
34 (U) Battalion Kings African Rifles
26 Infantry Brigade
HQ 26 Infantry Brigade
26 Infantry Brigade Signals Section Cipher Section & LAD
22 (NY) Battalion Kings African Rifles
36 (TT) Battalion Kings African Rifles
44 (U) Battalion Kings African Rifles
13 (NY) Battalion Kings African Rifles

20 INDIAN DIVISION

Headquarters
HQ 20 Indian Division
HQ Royal Artillery 20 Indian Division
HQ 20 Indian Division Engineers
HQ 20 Indian Division RIASC
HQ 20 Indian Division IEME
4 Madras less 1 platoon

Artillery
9 Field Regiment, Signals Section & LAD
114 (J) Field Regiment, Signals Section & LAD
53 AA/Anti Tank Regiment & Workshop Section
23 Indian Mountain Regiment & Signals Section

Engineers
92/422/481 Indian Field Companies
309 Indian Field Park Company
9 Indian Division Br Pl

Signals
20 Indian Division Signals

S.T.
37/38/39/45 Indian Comp Issue Secs.
100/102 Indian GPT Companies (15 cwt)
122 Indian GPT Company (3 tons)
628 Indian Supply Section
38 Bakery Section
3 Indian Field Ambulance Troop
14/30/43/52/55 Indian Mule Companies

Medical
42/55/59 Indian Field Ambulance Units
20 Indian Anti-Malaria Unit
26 Indian Field Hygiene Section

Pro
20 Indian Division Pro Unit

EME
63/64 Indian Mobile Workshop Companies
20 Indian Recovery Company

Int
604 Indian FS Section

Postal
76/120/122/123 Indian Field PO Units

Veterinarian
13 Indian Mobile Vet Section

Infantry
32 Indian Infantry Brigade
HQ 32 Indian Infantry Brigade
HQ 32 Indian Infantry Brigade Signals Section
HQ 32 Indian Infantry Brigade LAD (E)
1 Northamptonshire
9/14 Punjab
3/8 Punjab
80 Indian Infantry Brigade
HQ 80 Indian Infantry Brigade
HQ 80 Indian Infantry Brigade Signals Section
HQ 80 Indian Infantry Brigade LAD (E)
1 Devonshire

9 Frontier Field Force Regiment
3/1 Gurkha Rifles
100 Indian Infantry Brigade
HQ 100 Indian Infantry Brigade
HQ 100 Indian Infantry Brigade Signals Section
HQ 100 Indian Infantry Brigade LAD (E)
2 Border Regiment
14 Frontier Force Rifles
4/10 Gurkha Rifles
Platoon 4 Madras

23 INDIAN DIVISION

Headquarters
HQ 23 Indian Division
HQ 23 Indian Division Def & Empl Pl
HQ Royal Artillery 23 Indian Division
HQ 23 Indian Division Engineers
HQ 23 Indian Division RIASC
HQ 23 Indian Division IEME
2 Hyderabad

Artillery
158 (J) Field Regiment, Signals Section & LAD
3 Indian Field Regiment, Signals Section & LAD
28 Indian Mountain Regiment, Signals Section & LAD
2 Indian AA/Anti Tank Regiment, Signals Section & LAD

Engineers
2 Madras Engineer Battalion.
68/71/91 Indian Field Companies
323 Indian Field Park Company
10 Indian Div Br Pl
Section 442 Indian Quarrying Company

Signals
23 Indian Division Signals
3 Indian Cipher Section

S.T.
HQ 23 Indian Division Transport Section
21/24/50/61 Mule Companies

121/122/123 Indian GPT Companies
12/13/14/15 Indian Comp Issue Sections
7/10/18 Indian Field Ambulance Troops

Medical
24/47/49 Indian Field Ambulance
23 Indian Field Hygiene Section
68 AMU

Pro
23 Indian Division Pro Unit

EME
38/61 Indian Mobile Workshop Companies
1/37/49 Indian LAD Type 'E'
23 Indian Division Recovery Company
204 Wireless Workshop Section Type 'A'

Veterinarian
5 Indian Mobile Vet Section

Postal
69/91/99/117 Indian FPO

Misc
605 Indian FS Section
23 Indian Division Reinforcement Battalion

Infantry
1 Indian Infantry Brigade
HQ 1 Indian Infantry Brigade
HQ 1 Indian Infantry Brigade Signals Section
1 Seaforth Highlanders
1/16 Punjab
1 Patiala Infantry
37 Indian Infantry Brigade
HQ 37 Indian Infantry Brigade
HQ 37 Indian Infantry Brigade Signals Section
3/3 Gurkha Rifles
3/5 RGR
3/10 Gurkha Rifles
49 Indian Infantry Brigade

HQ 49 Indian Infantry Brigade
HQ 49 Indian Infantry Brigade Signals Section
4 Mahratta
6 Mahratta
5 Rajputana Rifles

253 SUB AREA

18 Mahratta
27 Mahratta
1 Chamar

256 SUB AREA

Kalibahadur Regiment

Appendix III

15th Army Order of Battle

Information from a Japanese *15th Army* Staff Table, dated 7 January 1945, captured at Meiktila March 1945.

	Code No.	Personnel
31 Division	RETSU 10720	
130 Infantry Regiment	RETSU 10353	1733
33 Division	YUMI 10722	
Divisional HQ	YUMI 6820	212
213 Infantry Regiment	YUMI 6822	464
214 Infantry Regiment	YUMI 6823	425
215 Infantry Regiment	YUMI 6824	564
33 Mountain Artillery Regiment	YUMI 6825	232
33 Engineer Regiment	YUMI 6826	249
Signals Unit	YUMI 6827	148
33 Transport Regiment	YUMI 6828	489
Ord Duty Unit	YUMI (formerly 6829)	84
Medical Unit	YUMI 6830	165
No. 1 Field Hospital	YUMI 6831	204
No. 2 Field Hospital	YUMI 6832	206
Vet depot	YUMI 6833	41
Water Purification Unit	YUMI (formerly 6834)	86
Attached Troops		
One infantry regiment of *53 Division*		
One Battalion 124 Infantry Regiment	8906	530
One WT platoon 19 Signals Regiment	10700	50
One platoon Shipping Engineer Regiment	1750	–
22 Bridging Material Company	1374	440
15 River Crossing Material Company	3964	240
335 Independent Motor Transport Company	12238	654
2 Company 3 Special Water Transport Regiment	10438	50
One platoon (less one detachment) YUMI of 30 Sea Duty Company	5194	189
21 Special Sea Duty Company	10393	52

One platoon (less one section)		
53 Construction Duty Company	6911	70
72 CCS (less one detachment – Tr)	6032	25
1 'Manufacture Materials' (SEI-SAI – Tr)		
Platoon less two sections		
No. 1 Transport Company, 1 Division, INA		17

Total strength *33 Division* and attached troops	5859

53 Division	YASU 10016	
151 Infantry Regiment	YASU 10022	850

No. of guns – 7 January 1945

31 Division

31 Mountain Artillery Regiment	6 mountain guns
	1 10cm howitzer

33 Division

Divisional HQ	2 Machine Guns
213 Infantry Regiment	4 Machine Guns
	1 Battalion gun
214 Infantry Regiment	4 Machine Guns
215 Infantry Regiment	5 Machine Guns
33 Division Mountain Artillery	4 mountain guns
33 Division Engineer Regiment	5 Machine Guns
33 Division Transport Regiment	2 Machine Guns

53 Division

151 Infantry Regiment	9 Machine Guns
	6 Anti Tank Guns
	2 Battalion guns
	3 Regimental guns

Comparative figures for Guns as at end of December 1944

33 Division

92 Type	35
92 Type Infantry Gun	11
94 Type Anti Tank Gun	5
41 Type Mountain Gun	2
94 Type Mountain Gun	7

Number of MT and AT in *15 Army*

33 Division

	205 MT
	283 AT

Appendix IV

Estimate of Japanese Losses

**Estimate of Japanese Personnel and Equipment losses during
the Meiktila campaign up to 9 March 1945**

(17 Indian Division Intelligence Summary)

Personnel

Killed	2251
Wounded	659*

*Definitely seen but total estimated at double this number.

Weapons Captured or Destroyed

Battalion guns Model '92'	70mm	8
Regimental guns Model '41'	75mm	9
Meiji Model '34' 2		
Mountain Guns Model '94'	75mm	4
Field Guns Model '38'	75mm	1
Field Guns	105mm	1
Anti Tank Guns Model '94'		16
Anti Tank Guns Mk. II	40mm	1
Anti Tank Guns Model '97'		6
AA/Anti Tank Guns Model '98'		3
AA Guns Model Model '88'	75mm	2
Tank guns	37mm	2
Tank guns	47mm	1
Mortars (including 1 British type)		5
Medium Machine Guns		34
Light Machine Guns		19
Anti Tank Rifles		7
Rifles		24**

**Captured but at least an additional 400 destroyed.

APPENDIX IV: ESTIMATE OF JAPANESE LOSSES

Vehicles

Motorcycle & sidecar	1
15 cwt lorry	2
3 ton lorries (including 1 six wheeler)	10
Tractors	8
Trailers	1
Cycles	1

Dumps

Food	8
Miscellaneous stores (artillery rangefinders, sights, signals telephones, handsets, wireless sets etc.)	15

Index